FATHERS
Raising
DAUGHTERS
(AFTER THE LOSS OF A SPOUSE)

Bruce D. Johnson

FATHERS
Raising Daughters After The
LOSS OF A SPOUSE

Bruce D. Johnson

JMPinckney Publishing Company, LLC
104 Berkeley Square Lane
PMB 28
Goose Creek, South Carolina 29445
Illustration and Design:
Printed in the United

Dedication

This spiritual journey would never have been complete without the love of my family and friends. Each time I felt the path of late-night research and writing, it became increasingly difficult; however, my daughters Brett and Maya, remained my motivation. My children are an abundant gift from God, and I am so thankful to have completed this journey so that I can biblically build a foundation for them to succeed in this world. I am very thankful for my parents, Alfred Sr. and Bernice Johnson, who gave me all of the necessary tools to chisel away the gates called obstacles and construct monuments of determination and perseverance. I am also grateful for my sisters and brothers, who provide me with continuous love and care for my children. I am surrounded by two wonderful aunts whom I feel would do anything for me. I feel truly blessed to have such God-fearing women by my side. My Aunt Sara celebrated her 83rd birthday on April 12th. My Aunt Laura Henri would have celebrated her 90th birthday on April 7th. These women of God have been with me since my marriage in 2004 to Dr. Maria Goodloe-Johnson. Whenever I was asked to speak or preach at an event or church, my aunts were there. When Maria and I moved to Seattle, Washington, my two aunts came across the country to visit. I can't say enough about how they have helped me through my spiritual journey and the journey of just living. God is Good all the time, and all the time, He is Good.

My spiritual coaches, Bishop William White, Brother Dallas Wilson, Rev. Dr. Jimmy Gallant, and Minister Francis Seabrook, as well as my entire church family, made sure that I was fueled with His daily bread to prevent my faith from depleting when my journey became tumultuous.

This entire manuscript is dedicated to my inspirational, encouraging, courageous, and dearest wife, Dr. Maria Goodloe-Johnson, who is now an angel that has taught me to sing, *"It is well, it is well, with my soul."*

Acknowledgments

I must give all thanks and glory to God for providing me with peace and patience to weather my many storms. The following scriptures not only summarize my earthly journey but are the instruments that I use to replenish my soul and build faith endurance:

Not that I speak in respect of want: for I have learned whatsoever state I am, therewith to be content. I know both how to be abased, and I know how to abound: everywhere and in all things, I am instructed both to be full and to be hungry, both to abound and to suffer need. I can do all things through Christ, which strengthened me.   Philippians 4:11-13 (NIV)

Therefore I take pleasure in infirmities, in reproaches, in necessities, in persecutions, in distresses for 'Christ's sake: for when I am weak, then am I strong.
2 Corinthians 12:10 (NIV)

Yea doubtless, and I count all things but loss for the excellency of the knowledge of

Christ Jesus my Lord: for whom I have suffered the loss of all things, and do count

them but dung, that I may win Christ.

Philippians 3:8 (NIV)

I am thankful for the partnership of my content specialist, Dr. Jacinta Bryant. Her guidance and support have been wonderful.

TABLE OF CONTENTS

Chapter One

Proverbs 22:6 tells the parent to train up a child in the way he should go: and when he is old, he will not depart from it. Parenting is a difficult task in the modern world. Although some aspects, such as physical work at home, have been simplified by technological advancements, the rise of digital media has necessitated parents to affirm values and practices more strongly to their children. This is challenging for a modern family with two parents who can take the time to reaffirm each other's position when one is not able to reinforce family education. The situation is even direr in single-parent families.

In many cases, single parents lack the resources and social support system necessary for raising a child. There are about 13.6 million single parents in the United States who are raising more than 24 million children (KID COUNT (2016, see Appendix A). "Once shunned by many churches as "sinners" and masters of their own downfall, the nation's 13 million single parents and their kids are increasingly being viewed as the widows and orphans Jesus tended in the bible" (Johnson, 2001).

Although social systems have rapidly accepted single-parent and female-led families, single-father-led families remain rare, and therefore, have more difficulties accessing social support. According to the U.S. Bureau of Statistics, about two million single fathers live in the United States. This accounts for about 17% of all single parents in the United States (KIDS COUNT, 2016). This figure is even more disproportionate in conservative states, such as South Carolina; therefore, it is rare to find single fathers in Charleston, South Carolina. During the 2012–2013 fiscal year, one of Charleston's homeless shelters served 358 single mothers as opposed to only eight single fathers. South Carolina area statistics show that 43% of the families in the state are headed by single parents (KIDS COUNT, 2016, see Appendix A).

Context of this Study

Protestant Episcopal Churches affiliated with the Diocese of South Carolina record approximately 22,000 baptized members spread across the state's east coast. The Diocese was founded in 1785 by the parishes of the former South Carolina colony. Based in the Lowcountry of South Carolina, the Diocese is one of the oldest religious districts in the United States. It includes several of the oldest operating churches in the nation. The Diocese dissociated from the Episcopal Church in the fall of 2012.

The Diocese of South Carolina is recognized by Anglican Dioceses and Provinces worldwide, many of whom have broken fellowship with The Episcopal Church. In 2013, the Diocese joined the global Fellowship of Confessing Anglicans and entered a formal relationship of Provisional Primatial Oversight with Global South Primates. The Diocese of South Carolina includes faithful Anglicans under the leadership of Right Reverend Mark J. Lawrence, the 14th Bishop of the Diocese. Pursuing the vision first cast in his message at the 2009 Diocesan Convention, Bishop Lawrence urged the Christian community to focus on "Making Biblical Anglicans for a Global Age." According to Bishop Lawrence, continuing this mission involves the Diocese, "To respond to the Great Commission by so presenting Jesus Christ in the power of the Holy Spirit that all may come to know Him as Savior and follow Him as Lord in the fellowship of His Church."(Lawrence, 2009).

Research Question

The following question guided the research in this study: What support systems are available in the Protestant Episcopal Church in the Diocese of South Carolina for fathers raising daughters after losing a spouse?

Theory

This project was built on the premise that the church is an integral part of society. Although the church's primary role is to facilitate a form of conversion for eternal life, it cannot ignore the human plight. Life on earth is a prerequisite for the attainment of eternal life. Some theologians have argued that the sharp decline in religious participation is attributed to the detached form of worship that insists on moralistic piety without any practical relevance (Van Biema, 2007).

Apart from its spiritual obligation, the church is also advantageously positioned to solve the two challenges of single-parenting and grief-management (Johnson, 2000). Grief can affect the entirety of the Christian mission. When a person dies, the Christian belief is that the individual has transitioned into a better existence; however, the bereavement causes tremendous grief and sadness for the Christian family experiencing the loss of a loved one.

A primary goal of the church is to bring hope in a period that may be accompanied by disillusionment and despair. In all of an individual's associations, the church possesses the possibility of delivering a positive message. Church leaders and members must congregate around a grieving person to offer both tangible and emotional support. With an awareness of the difficulty an individual is facing, the role of the church is to assess and monitor the needs of the family. An assessment may include taking care of the children to give them an opportunity to retreat, offering to care for children through advice and counseling, and providing parents with ministries within the church that can occupy their time (Children's Trust of South Carolina, 2016).

Goal of the Grief Ministry Project

Considering the support of the church in times of grief, with a specific interest in the needs of single fathers, the goal of this study was to explore and more fully understand the lived experience and perceptions of the support provided by the church for fathers raising daughters after the death of a spouse in the Protestant Episcopal Church in the Diocese of South Carolina. Ultimately, such a goal would lead the church to develop and implement grief ministry support systems within the Protestant Episcopal Diocese of South Carolina for single male parents raising daughters after the death of their spouse.

Chapter Two

Spiritual Autobiography

...I have learned, in whatsoever state I am, therewith to be content.
I know both how to be abased, and I know how to abound:
everywhere and in all things, I am instructed both to be full and to be hungry,
both to abound and to suffer need. I can do all things through
Christ, which strengtheneth me.
Philippians 4:12

This quote from Philippians constantly reminds me that wherever I am, whatever I am experiencing, and with whoever is on my life's path, I am contented. This bible passage affirms that I am exactly where I am supposed to be, and thus there is no need for me to be anxious, worried, stressed out, or unsure about anything. Through Christ, who strengthens me, I am contented. Being able to embrace, believe, and live my life this way is a result of a lifelong spiritual journey.

My life's spiritual journey – beginning from an awareness of Jesus at a very young age, commitment to conversion and accepting Jesus as my Savior, surviving profound loss, and a call to ministry, to a spiritual life of contentment, affirmed on a daily basis through my actions, words, and thoughts -- has led me to a sacred place of unwavering faith in the Lord Jesus Christ. Today my belief in God is enduring -- no matter what tumultuous times may occur or what physical or material things may languish or flourish during this, my earthly existence. While I have come to understand throughout my life that I simply need to maintain my faith and do the footwork so that God's Will and plans for me will unfold, this was not always the case. Although regular prayer, church services, and God have been a mainstay in my life since childhood, my personal spiritual core, as it is today, developed and deepened as a direct result of decades of life events – some celebratory, some sorrow-filled. My human spirit has been fueled, strengthened, tested, renewed, and inspired by specific places, people, and experiences in my life throughout the years.

Places That Have Contributed to My Spiritual Growth

The neighborhood churches: While every community has some form of religious worship, not every child gets the opportunity to explore and experience organized prayer and celebration at their local church. Suppose a parent, grandparent, or other devoutly religious relative do not purposefully make Sunday services or Sunday school attendance as a norm in a child's family? In that case, the opportunity for that youngster to make God an integral part of his/her life at an early age is gone. I was blessed to have parents who were committed to each other, to our family, and to God. I was blessed to have God-fearing aunts and grandparents who were a regular presence in my childhood years. Without these key members of my family, surely my life's choices would have taken me down another road – on a completely different journey where anyone without any spirituality or religious beliefs may have influenced me.

Though I did not realize it at the time, the underpinning of my spiritual journey began when I was just six years old at a church just three blocks from my home – thanks to the direction, spirituality, and commitment of my family members. This was the first church I was going to; it was also where I attended Sunday school and first learned about Jesus. I loved Sunday school. Unlike many other children in my neighborhood, I looked forward to attending Sunday school each week – always wondering what new story I would hear about Jesus or what new project we would be working on that connected to that week's scriptures. The Pastor at that local church was always so kind to everyone. He was knowledgeable about Jesus; his stories brought the bible to life for me. He always made it seem that Jesus was easy to know and easy to welcome into one's life.

Although I was often teased by the neighborhood kids either because I was the tallest one in the Sunday school class or because my clothes never seemed to be able to keep up with my growth spurts, it never stopped me from looking forward to each Sunday's lessons at this local church. While the studies about Jesus when I was just six became the foundation for what was to be a life of prayer, religious devotion, and spirituality in the decades to follow, as a young, wide-eyed boy, I did not realize just how much I would remember from those Sunday school sessions. I did not realize at the time just how much I would emulate what I was taught back then, to one day be a part of what I was going to teach others when I led Sunday school students. Later in my life, when I was an adult, I served as a Pastor and had young, wide-eyed neighborhood children in my church who usually came for Sunday school; I always fondly reflected on my own experiences as a child at my local church; I wanted the church where I served to ignite those same feelings of authentic curiosity, interest, and enthusiasm for Jesus in the youngsters attending my church's Sunday school.

When I became a young adult, I was ordained as a Eucharistic Lay Minister. As a Eucharistic Lay Minister, I was humbled and honored to be given the responsibility of distributing communion during service. This role also enabled me to bring the Eucharist to the homebound in my community. It was during this experience that I really felt like I was being of service to others. As I visited the homebound, I was able to share scripture from the services, news about the church, and ask the individuals about themselves. It was a beautiful connection -- with the Eucharist at the center of it all -- with many seniors and other homebound members of our church community. During this experience, I also realized just how many people in the neighborhood of a local church are in need of so much. I prayed that other young adults in my church would long to reach out to the needy, as well. When I shared my stories and experiences with my peers, I knew that my passion and commitment as a Eucharistic Lay Minister always came through. As a result, my actions, deeds, and words inspired some of my friends to want to be Eucharistic Lay Ministers, as well.

Beyond that little local church just a few blocks from my childhood home, there were other churches in my community that also helped to develop my spiritual life.

People Who Have Contributed to My Spiritual Growth

Two parents, two-paths to church: My parents went to different churches when I was a young boy. My mother faithfully attended the local African Methodist Episcopal (AME) Church, while my father went to an Episcopal Anglican Church in the neighborhood. Growing up in a household where both of my parents each attended completely different churches with completely different approaches to celebrating their religion is significant in my spirituality and how I chose to influence and inspire my children. While I eventually attended the churches of both of my parents throughout the years, it was an experience that I knew I did not want to repeat for my daughters when my second wife and I each gravitated towards two different churches.

Growing up, there were six children in my household. As my siblings and I got older, my parents started taking us to church with them. When my siblings went with my mom to her African Methodist Episcopal Church, I headed out with my dad to the local Episcopal Church. I was thrilled. I loved doing things with my dad, and I loved how passionate and committed my father was to his faith. I was proud to be at his side during those Sunday services.

My father often shared stories with me about his church. Many of these stories stuck with me throughout the years. I learned that it was the same exact church that he attended when he was a little boy of my age, the same church that his mother attended at the time, and the same church that his maternal grandmother attended, as well. My presence at the church made it four generations of our family praising God in that same one church. I thought of my grandparents a lot when I prayed, sang, and sat in that church with my dad. I was proud to attend the same church to which my grandmother and her mother belonged.

Though my siblings eventually stopped attending church regularly with our mother, my grandmother insisted that I continued to attend church with her and my dad. I remained faithful to my local church throughout my young life. As I grew up and moved out of the neighborhood, however, I attended other churches. I did not return to my grandmother and father's Episcopal Church until I was an adult. It was a church that I would always go back to, which had profound meaning in my life. It was my great-grandmother's church, my grandmother's church, my father's church, and my church. It was the Episcopal Church where I formally accepted Jesus as my Lord and Savior, and it was the first church where I became very active in the church service.

As I became older, I also attended church services with my mother. Normally, my mom and my siblings would attend the first Sunday service at the African Methodist Episcopalian (AME) church on Wadmalaw Island. I loved the First Sundays. They reminded me of being at a gospel concert whenever the Senior Choir would sing hymns. I have met churchgoers throughout my life who do not care for music or a choir during the service. To me, a choir is so full of the Holy Spirit. In fact, during many services with my mother and my siblings at her church, the members would be so moved by the choir that they would get up out of their seats and dance. My brothers, sisters, and I were so amazed and in awe of witnessing this celebratory praise that we did not move.

In addition to the congregation dancing and singing and praising the Lord for all to witness, the members would begin to speak in a language that did not make any sense to my siblings and me. This language was not the English dialect. As I became better acquainted with my mother's church, I discovered the members were "speaking in tongue." This behavior was so different from the Episcopal Anglican Church that I regularly attended with my father and my paternal grandmother. The Episcopal Anglican Church is known as the "frozen chosen" because of the way they remain quiet during service. In the Episcopal Church, the congregation uses the Book of Common Prayer, which outlines the order of service. Attending services with my mother at her church was beautiful and inspiring. I had the opportunity to witness and come to understand firsthand that there are more ways than one to praise and honor the Lord. I was so used to the Episcopal Anglican Church that I attended so often with my father that being a part of what my mother experienced on Sundays meant a great deal to me, as well. This experience and realization have remained with me throughout my life.

My paternal grandmother: My paternal grandmother was the matriarch of the family; she was the voice of the family. She was deeply respected and loved by everyone in the family. She lived just two blocks behind our home, making it convenient and easy for me to spend time with her when I was a young boy. My grandmother's steadfast devotion to the church and her active involvement in her church was the thread that kept all of us tightly drawn to church as well – especially me. She encouraged and inspired me to be an active member of the church's congregation and not simply a member who attended services once a week and then left. As a result, I was her only grandchild who consistently attended church and got involved with various youth programs.

As I got older and had a better understanding and a clearer perspective of others, I came to realize that my grandmother saw a kind and gentle spirit in me that I could not see or recognize in myself when I was younger. Because of her, I grew to love church, the fellowship, and all the activities that I participated in during those very early formative years. My paternal grandmother was a lead-by-example devoted child of God. Through her words, actions, and choices, she showed me how to live as a Christian person.

My first wife and the mother of daughter : After I graduated from high school, I attended Trident Technical College. During that time, I applied for and secured a job at UPS. Working for UPS was a big deal; everyone knew they offered great benefits and a great salary. While working at UPS, I met the woman that was to become my first wife and the mother of my daughter. Having my own family as an integral part of my extended family brought me even closer to God and my spirituality. I felt blessed to be a father and wanted to be the best husband and father I could. Unfortunately, I was young and did not realize I had a lot more to learn about compromising and communicating effectively with a spouse.

The first major loss in my life was not the death of a loved one but a divorce. During the first five years of our relationship, everything seemed great! However, after the fifth year, we could never seem to agree on anything – especially anything related to our home or how we wanted to parent our daughter, Brett. When we married before God and our family and friends, I thought it was for our lifetime. I never imagined I would be divorced. It conflicted with everything I believed in during my upbringing in both my home and my church. After seeking advice from professional marriage counselor and a spiritual counselor, my wife and I separated and later got a divorce. At that time, my daughter was just in the 2nd grade. When my first wife moved out of the area with Brett, it became logistically challenging for me to be a regular, consistent part of my daughter's daily life. Nonetheless, I made it a point to talk with her often and remained a mainstay in her life. This loss in my life, family, and daughter's daily life was incredibly sad and emotional. I felt broken. In hindsight, I realized that I spent too much time worrying about and trying to figure out what I was going to do next instead of turning it all over to God and God's Will; I just focused on being the best father and person I could be. I wasted so much time squabbling over insignificant, meaningless material things with my ex-wife while dividing what belonged to me and what belonged to her. It seemed to take us forever to agree on when was the best time for each of us to be with our daughter individually. I finally came to my spiritual senses and realized that everything was going to be ok and that through Christ, I would be strengthened and renewed again. As devastating and disappointing as this break-up was in my family, I continued to be active in my church. Although I did not know it at the time, a few years later, I was to experience another profound loss in my personal life.

My second wife and my daughter: On September 26, 2004, I was blessed with marrying a wonderful woman, Maria Goodloe. I felt refreshed and renewed. I was ready for a change in my religious life and lovingly agreed to join the United Methodist Church with my wife. The United Methodist Church is where my second wife was a member at an early age; in fact, she had been a member all her life. My wife grew up in the United Methodist Church. Our daughter, Maya, was also christened in this church. It was important to me to worship together as a family and not try to attend two different churches like my parents did. Although I had the opportunity to witness how different churches celebrate and praise God by attending two different churches with my parents, I wanted a different experience for Maya. I wanted her to have a solid foundation in a church with both of her parents at her side each week.

Attending this church with my wife and daughter enabled me to meet many wonderful people who inspired me to be even more involved with the church. In fact, it was Maria's pastor, Reverend Sam Johnson, at the United Methodist Church in Mount Pleasant, South Carolina, who helped steer me into following my heart and pursuing my calling in the ministry. This calling remains vivid in my life.

Reverend Sam was a passionate and powerful speaker. I was moved by his sermons. He did not just talk about the scriptures; he brought them to life. He encouraged and inspired the members of the congregation to take action – to get involved. His spirit was a connection that I will never forget. His ability to make the scripture and life stories of Jesus so real in his teachings that they stayed with me long after the service was over. He ended every sermon with a Negro Spiritual that sealed the story. Reverend Sam passed away a couple of years after we moved away. I miss Reverend Sam, but his impact and memory are forever a part of my Christian calling. I know that God put him on my life's path for a reason. Had I never divorced my first wife and married my second wife, I would never have attended the United Methodist Church in Mount Pleasant, and I would never have met Reverend Sam. I realize now that when we go through tumultuous times that seem unbearable and confusing, other people and experiences come into our lives that transform us and inspire us into becoming the best version of ourselves, where we can then be of greater service to others.

Three years after Maria and I married, we relocated from Charleston to Seattle for her new role as the Superintendent of Seattle Public Schools. When we moved to Seattle, it was the first time in my life that I had moved so far away from my family, friends, church, and community in Charleston. Although Maria and I were excited and ready to begin our journey in Seattle, it was difficult to adjust to being in a brand new location – especially one so different from Charleston. The first several years were extremely challenging. I found myself wanting to go home for my birthdays, holidays, summer breaks, the Spoleto Arts Festival, and all other community events.

As much as I missed my life in Charleston, my religious life in Seattle was very fulfilling. Maria and I decided we were going to worship in Seattle at an Episcopal church. I felt worshiping at an Episcopal Church would help us to remain a strong Christian family. My family and I found a church we liked very much and where we worshiped on Sundays and special occasions.

My teenage daughter, Maya: Being a father is an honor and a gift from God. It strengthens my spirituality in ways that would not be if I did not have Maya. I am responsible for her well-being – physically, spiritually, intellectually, and emotionally. I pray every day that I can raise her in a way that is pleasing to our Heavenly Father and in a way that would make her mother proud. The bible says in Proverbs 22:6 --*Train up a child in the way he or (she) should go, and he (she) will not depart from it.* I pray the things that I am instilling in her today; she will be able to use as a stepping-stone to be successful in the future – just like my father and family members did for me. I truly believe that if a person tries to do what is right and teach the child the difference between good and evil, God will guide the child toward the right path.

While my ministerial skills have increased and improved throughout the years, the one thing that I was not prepared for was adjusting to being the father of a strong-willed, opinionated, bright, and beautiful teenage daughter! Wow, this was a big surprise for me. Everything was different. Things like going to the mall, purchasing clothes for her, and taking her to the beautician to get her hair braided. When Maya was in elementary school, I was curling her hair before she went to school. This quickly came to an end once Maya entered middle school. Maya was insistent about her independence and preferred that I gave her the liberty to be more responsible for her own needs. Not only has her independence increased, but Maya has grown four inches within a year, from sixth to seventh grade. It has truly been an amazing journey and blessing watching my daughter transition from a child to a teenager. I share stories with her about how I got involved in my church as a young teenager, and I encourage her to explore the different services and activities available to the youth at our church.

How Formal Education Further Developed My Spirituality

After my divorce from my first wife, I decided to go back to college and finish my degree. Since I had dedicated years of my life to UPS, I decided to major in Organizational Management with hopes that a formal degree in this field would spark a renewed interest and passion for my career with UPS. I attended Voorhees College in Denmark, South Carolina. Since I only had a few courses to complete my undergraduate degree, I embraced the unique opportunity to live on campus in my own dorm room. During this time in my life, I met Fr. Johnson – the Chaplain at the college. Fr. Johnson took me under his wings. He became a wonderful mentor and inspiration to me, from providing me with dinner in the evenings when I missed the opportunity to go to dinner on campus to help me to focus on becoming an inspirational person to sharing my thoughts and goals. Fr. Johnson was the reason I was meant to wait until I was 37 years old to complete my degree!

Had I earned my college degree in four years right after high school, I would never have met him. Through his role at the college, I further understood, appreciated, and became excited about the role of ministry in a community. Fr. Johnson gave me the opportunity to work with him in the college chapel, where all students at the college were required to attend services once a week. I helped Fr. Johnson prepare for the services; I lit candles, directed students where to sit, and became a lay reader during many services. I helped him with funerals, and he took me around the campus and the community with him as he provided ministry services to others. The chapel was my home away from home. When I graduated from Voorhees College, I became the first UPS full-time employee in Charleston to earn a college degree.

During my first few years married to Maria, I was still working at UPS; I was there for over 23 years. Though I was happily married, I continued to feel a void in my life, both professionally and personally. I knew something was missing in my life, but I could not put my finger on the problem. This void I was experiencing was a constant and increasing need to be a part of the church in a way that gave back to my community. After talking with my Maria and praying over it,

I decided to visit a seminary in Columbia, South Carolina -- 127 miles from Charleston. Going on for my Master's in Theology meant that I would be relinquishing my role with the United Parcel Service. Although (UPS) was a good company to work for, and I really worked hard driving the brown truck; however, I was seeking and searching for something else. That something else was serving God. I did try to suppress that feeling for a long time, but it came at a time in my life where I had to face my inner feelings. It was hard because it was painful to think about losing or walking away from a good job with great benefits, a good salary, and fantastic retirement benefits. It was hard, but when I think about the goodness of Jesus, there is no job, no paid vacation, and no benefits that are better than God's plan for our lives.

After visiting the seminary and sitting in on several classes, I was excited about the experience. I enjoyed being in a classroom environment where everyone wanted to participate and learn more about our Lord and Savior, Jesus Christ. During the middle of my first semester at the seminary, my wife was asked to interview for the position of Superintendent for Seattle Public Schools. She was offered the job, and we later moved to Seattle, Washington. In Seattle, I was able to finish my Master's in Theology – an area of focus that was so meaningful and interesting to me.

Significant Loss That Has Contributed to My Spiritual Growth

In addition to places of worship, individuals in my life, and my formal education all being profound factors that have contributed to the spiritual person I am today, the losses I have experienced have also affected my life. While I have experienced the death of three significant people in my life – two of those deaths affirmed my faith and gratitude for the people who brought me closer to God, and the other one left me at a crossroads where I could have easily – in my profound grief and overwhelming despair -- chosen the wrong path at that junction in my life.

The death of my grandmother: My grandmother's death – a few years after my divorce from my first wife -- was the first death of a loved one in my life that affected me. When my grandmother passed away a few years after I was divorced, it caused a huge void in my spiritual life; however, I never left the church, I never stopped believing in Jesus Christ, and I never stopped praying. I know many people who become angry with God or even stop believing in God when they lost a loved one. That was not an option for me. My faith sustained me.

When my paternal grandmother died, it affected me deeply because we were so very close and because it was her spirituality, her religious foundation, and her commitment to her church that influenced and inspired me at such a young age. Despite having lost my grandmother that was such a huge presence in my daily life when I was a child *and* an adult, I ran toward God instead of away from Him. By continuing to show up – physically – for church services, I began to heal. Though I will always miss my grandmother dearly, I can still clearly hear her voice and direction on a regular basis, and she is still a part of my life.

The death of my second wife: The second significant loss in my life that impacted my spirituality was also the death of a loved one – my second wife. After years in Seattle, we relocated to Detroit, Michigan, where Maria was recruited for another leadership role in education. It was while we were in Michigan that Maria was diagnosed with lung cancer. I was shocked, scared, and worried, all at the same time. This was the most significant loss in my life and the only time where everything I had been trained, inspired, and encouraged to do, to think, to trust, and to believe in -- went out the window.

While I knew that I had my strong connection to God to depend on, it did not seem to ease the sorrow and sadness and the fear of losing my beloved wife. Fortunately, I was surrounded by friends who are Christians and who also believe in the power of prayer and in God. After a couple of months of chemotherapy, the doctors informed us that the treatment was not working. I decided to take Maria to Houston, Texas, to the University of Texas M.D. Anderson Cancer Center -- one of the best cancer treatment centers in the world. During this stressful and emotional time, God continued to provide; He put wonderful, compassionate people on our life's path who helped us when we needed it most. We were blessed to be able to stay with the Smith family we knew in Texas during our visit to M.D. Anderson. They opened their home to us and surrounded us with their Christian love and prayers; it was an incredible, spiritually-inspiring journey of faith, hope, and unconditional love. I felt blessed to call David my friend and bother from another mother.

During this time, I prayed not for an understanding of God's Will but rather – that the doctors at M.D. Anderson would be able to prescribe a treatment plan for my wife that would eradicate the cancer. On December 5, 2012, Maria went home to be with our Heavenly Father. I know God is always with us, no matter how hard

or difficult the situation may be. As heart-wrenching and emotional as it was trying

to find our way through Maria's life-threatening illness, the experience brought our

family closer to each other and closer to God. I will always remember and cherish

Maria's warm smile and contagious laugh.

The death of my father: The other loss that strengthened my faith was

when my father passed away in 2016. It was through my father's commitment to

his mother's and his grandmother's church that enabled me to experience that, too,

during my formidable years. My father was a role model to me – in both his

spiritual life and in his personal life. I learned from my father never to give up on

my dreams and desires. He taught me the importance and necessity of making

sacrifices to reach the personal and professional goals I have set in my life. My

father taught me how to live a life as a moral man of integrity and trustworthiness,

commitment, and kindness. I know that my aspiration to be an effective spiritual

leader was inspired by my father and will significantly help me become a good

priest or pastor -- wherever God leads me. Everywhere I travel, I am constantly

reminded of my grandmother and my father – of the activities they were involved with in the church and how I readily embraced the opportunities to be involved in church, too. While I think of my father and grandmother, I often know that they are watching over me.

Pastoral Work That Has Contributed to My Spiritual Growth

After the passing of my Maria, I decided to return to Detroit, where I was appointed pastor of a United Methodist Church. Four months later, I was asked to be the pastor at another United Methodist Church. After serving for five months at this church, I decided to move back to Charleston, South Carolina, where my family members could help take care of my daughter. I especially wanted her to be logistically close to our family during her young years and transitioning years into her teens. Since returning home, I have been actively involved with the youth group at my church.

While attending my home church, I participated in many roles. I served as a Sunday School Teacher. As a Sunday School Teacher, I embraced the opportunity to share some of the same wonderful insights and experiences I had with the youth of our church when I was attending Sunday school at the age of six. As I wrote and planned my lessons for each week, I prayed for inspiration and direction to present the children with what they needed to know, hear and understand on that particular Sunday. When their little hands went up with questions during the classes, I knew I was doing a good job because the children were thinking, reasoning, and questioning. It was a wonderful experience.

I also sang in the choir. Still moved and inspired by what I had experienced at my mother's church, I readily embraced the opportunity to be a part of my church's choir. Learning new hymns, practicing with other church members, and feeling a sense of community with them in bringing the Holy Spirit to the congregation as I had experienced, was a wonderful way to be of service to my fellow church members.

Another role I embraced was that of Youth Adviser. Even while I was growing up as a young boy in my neighborhood, I knew that not all of my friends came from homes where both of their parents lived together or where their grandparents lived nearby. As a Youth Adviser, I was able to serve as the lead-by-example role model for the youth in our community. For those who did not have a fatherly figure in their daily lives, I was able to show them -- through my actions, words, and faith – that despite where they may have come from, they can make choices to lead them down a healthy, Christ-centered path where they, too, can become contributing members of society.

In addition, I have started a Sunday school program at my home church which is Episcopal Anglican. I realize having faith in God has tightened the bond that my daughter and I share together and has made us stronger. While I am grateful I had the opportunity to work in Detroit as a pastor, and I know that I can transfer that experience to become a better preacher in the Episcopal Anglican church, I am happy to be back home with my family. My experience as a pastor in Detroit has truly strengthened my skills as a minister in the Anglican Church. My skillset as a preacher has also helped me develop better relationships with my friends, family, and church members. I find that many in my social circle have been faced with hardships, and I am able to provide ministerial and biblical support.

My Spirituality Today

My feeling about God as the center of my life is very good. I feel without having God in my life, I would be totally lost. I would be confused, misguided, and focused on things of the world that are useless and not important. I am not only a God-fearing man, but I am a man aspiring to teach other people and share the good news about our Lord and Savior. I know if it were not for His grace and mercy, I would not be here today. God is truly good. I thank God every day for allowing me to be here.

I am proud to be a Christian. I am the fourth generation to be associated with Episcopal affiliation. As of today, I have completed my Doctor of Ministry. I had to share my spiritual experience every step of the way when I was pursuing my B.S. degree, my master's, and my doctorate. This has been a long spiritual journey. Sometimes I feel upset and depressed thinking about my grandmother, my wife, and my father not being able to be here physically with me to share my joys and accomplishments. I know they are watching over me and smiling from heaven. God has blessed me with the ability to think clearly and use my hands. I plan on thinking and using my hands to build His kingdom on earth. If you believe and follow His ways, everything is possible.

Steadfast Faith in God

I am currently a Postulant for Presbyter. In the Anglican / Episcopal tradition, this means the candidate or Postulant are tested as a vocation to an ordained ministry or the religious life. Postulants for Presbyter seek ordination as deacon or priest. The length of postulancy varies. The time involves meeting with the bishop of the diocese, examination by the Commission on Ministry, along with physical and mental examinations, and in some cases --attending discernment class on the weekend. Postulancy is an initial time of preparation and testing for ordained ministry. Candidacy is the next stage in the ordination process. Many believe to be a priest in the Anglican / Episcopal Church, you must jump through hoops, and the process is long. I feel truly blessed to be a candidate for Presbyter, and my steadfast faith ensures me that everything will work out as God has planned for me.

It is Well with My Soul

My journey has been rough and has kept me up many nights. Through everything I have endured, experienced, and come to understand, I believe God is preparing me for the next chapter in my life. I know it is something great and right in sync with my lifelong commitment to and passion for ministry and serving the Lord. Through loss and disappointment and the death of loved ones, His grace and mercy have carried me when I could not carry myself. Scripture has assured me that "For from his fullness we have all

received grace upon grace." John 1:16.

I am further reminded of His grace every time I listen to the song "It Is Well With My Soul" by Horatio Spafford. This song served as a response to Horatio's faith after losing five children. Horatio was a wealthy businessman during the 1800s. Four of his children died while traveling on a ship with their mother to England. To inform Horatio of this tragedy, his wife sent him a telegram, "saved alone, what shall I do?"

While traveling to England to meet his grieving wife, the captain of the ship let Horatio know that they were passing over the spot where his four girls drowned. Horatio responded by writing this song:

It Is Well with My Soul

When peace like a river attendeth my way,

When sorrows like sea billows roll

Whatever my lot, thou hast taught me to say

It is well, it is well, with my soul.

It is well

With my soul

It is well, it is well with my soul

Though Satan should buffet, though trials should come,

Let this blest assurance control,

That Christ has regarded my helpless estate,

And hath shed His own blood for my soul

It is well (it is well)

With my soul (with my soul)

It is well, it is well with my soul

My sin, oh, the bliss of this glorious thought

My sin, not in part but the whole,

Is nailed to the cross, and I bear it no more,

Praise the Lord, praise the Lord, o my soul

It is well (it is well)

With my soul (with my soul)

It is well, it is well with my soul

It is well (it is well)

With my soul (with my soul)

It is well, it is well with my soul

Horatio Spafford (1876).

Chapter Three

Context and Praxis

The Episcopal Protestant Church in Charleston, South Carolina, is a neighbor to historical plantations that my enslaved ancestors cultivated in the 1800s. Begun as a small chapel on the grounds of a plantation in 1845 (Porwoll, 2014), the chapel was built by the plantation owner to teach slaves about the Gospel. This chapel was one of two places where slaves could worship. "Black communicants in the parish outnumbered Whites more than 8 to 1 (an average of 161 to 19) and accounted for one-fourth of the total in the entire diocese".

To date, my church remains on the original plantation site where it once was a chapel and is one of two predominantly Black churches within the Episcopal Protestant Church. Our enrollment has largely declined, but our ministry remains intact. We are aligned with the mission of our diocese, which is "to respond to the Great Commission by so presenting Jesus Christ in the power of the Holy Spirit that all may come to know Him as Savior and follow Him as Lord in the fellowship of His Church" (Diocese of South Carolina webpage, 2017).

If a person is traveling fast, he or she could miss seeing the church that is located off of the main highway in an area known as West of the Ashley. The members who attend church service on Sunday mornings are mostly African Americans. My grandmother began taking my siblings and me to church with her when we were in elementary school. Somewhere along the way, my siblings stopped going to church, and I found myself going with my grandmother alone. I grew to love going to church and serving God. I was baptized and confirmed in this church, where I have been a member for more than 40 years.

To date, my church remains a large congregation with many different activities going on during the week, in addition to Sunday services. The church went through some difficult times 35 years ago, including a fire that burned down the edifice. Following that, some of the church members did not agree with the priest, and more than half of the members left, including members of my immediate family, to form a Baptist congregation. My grandmother and I, along with a handful of other members, decided to stay. It was considered a family church, though I really did not understand what that meant until the separation. The members who left the church were the members who participated in different church activities and ministries and were members who were there when something needed to be fixed. In addition to their service, the members who left were tithers, whose contributions financially supported the ministry. The loss of those members led to a large decline in membership.

I was saddened because all the friends I had become accustomed to seeing and playing with on Sundays were gone. I am so glad I had a grandmother who decided that we were not leaving the church. I learned during that time that church was God's house and scripture became the focal point in my life. According to Matthew 18:15-17:

> *If your brother sins, go and show him his fault in private; if he listens to you, you have won your brother. But if he does not listen to you, take one or two more with you so that by the mouth of two or three witnesses, every fact may be confirmed. If he refuses to listen to them, tell it to the church; and if he refuses to listen even to the church, let him be to you as a Gentile and a tax collector.*

My grandmother told me to always try to talk about whatever bothered me and work it out. Although I stopped attending my former church in 2004 and attended a United Methodist Church with my wife in Seattle, Washington, I kept the congregation close to my heart. After the death of my wife, I relocated to Charleston in 2013 and returned to my original church, where my grandmother introduced me to the love of Christ. Even now, the church seems to be doing a little better because we serve an awesome God with whom everything is possible.

In the past 12 years, the church has had more than five different priests. This was difficult for the older members who wanted to have someone who knew them and whom they could trust. The medium age of people who attend the church is 35. The congregation includes children in grade school, middle school, young adults, and senior citizens. The socioeconomic composition includes retirees and the working middle class.

I believe the strength of the church is that they have learned how to work together, even during times of uncertainty and strife. Before I left Charleston, I thought the church was not going to survive financially or spiritually. Visitors were not welcomed, there was only one service during the week, and the sermons lasted for 20 minutes or less. I am reminded by Isaiah 41:10 to *"not fear, for I am with you; Do not anxiously look about you, for I am your God. I will strengthen you, surely I will help you. Surely I will uphold you with My righteous right hand."*

At the present time, it is exciting to see the rebirth that has taken place at my church. God has been good to me, and I want to use my gifts to serve or to give something back to God. I am the Christian Education Department superintendent, which provides oversight of the children's ministry, bible study, and Sunday school. In the Episcopal Church, the senior warden, junior warden, treasurer, and secretary provide oversight of the church. Decisions are usually made with the priest and the senior warden present. The congregation assists the senior warden in choosing members of the vestry, the church's governing body that represents the church during annual conferences.

All churches have some areas that can use some of God's grace and mercy. We are all guilty of blaming someone or talking about something that went on in the church. We often forget that no one except Jesus is perfect, and we know what happened to him. If they crucified Jesus, we all need to be on our knees in prayer. In Luke 22:39-46, Jesus also knelt in prayer:

And he came out and went, as was his custom, to the Mount of Olives, and the disciples followed him. And when he came to the place, he said to them, Pray that you may not enter into temptation. And he withdrew from them about a stone's throw, and knelt down and prayed, saying, Father, if you are willing, remove this cup from me. Nevertheless, not my will, but yours, be done. And there appeared to him an angel from heaven, strengthening him. And being in agony he prayed more earnestly, and his sweat became like great drops of blood falling down to the ground. And when he rose from prayer, he came to the disciples and found them sleeping for sorrow, and he said to them, Why are you sleeping? Rise and pray that you may not enter into temptation.

Ministry Praxis

I moved back to Charleston, South Carolina, on December 19, 2013. Before relocating to Charleston, my daughter and I lived in Detroit, Michigan, where I was the pastor of a United Methodist Church. Returning to Charleston, I felt a need to be involved in the church I was attending. I spoke to the priest about assisting with the ministry, and soon I was asked to be the Sunday School Superintendent. I am thankful that the priest of the Episcopal Anglican Church has allowed me to be a member of the ministry and to share my ideas and my message to the youth on Sunday mornings.

As a believer, I can certainly inspire others, especially our youth, who are faced with so many social pressures that overwhelmingly affect their emotional stability. This weakness often causes our youth to stray in negative directions. The young Christians that I am developing on Sunday mornings could be great examples to others. As Scripture reminds our youth, *"don't let anyone look down on you because you are young, but set an example for the believers in speech, in conduct, in love, in faith, and in purity"* (1 Timothy 4:12). My goal is to ensure that our youth understand that fitting in is not as important as taking a brave stand to exemplify what a relationship with Jesus looks like.

My Philosophy in Ministry

I believe God has a purpose for everyone, and I believe we all are created in His image to love, care for and help our neighbors. When we are able to treat our neighbors the same way we would like to be treated, God continues to shine His glory on us. God has given certain talents to each one of us to use while we are here on earth. If we truly believe in God's words and follow him in the ways and the guidelines that have been established for us, I believe God will direct our paths and be with us until we are called home to receive our reward. I feel that God calls me to lead, and help His people from pain and suffering in any way I can. God will not leave us or forsake us because of the love he has for all of us. This is even revealed by David to his son, Solomon:

> *Be strong and of good courage, and do [it]: fear not, nor be dismayed: for the LORD God, [even] my God, [will be] with thee; he will not fail thee, nor forsake thee, until thou hast finished all the work for the service of the house of the LORD* (1 Chronicles 28:20).

How I exercise my Philosophy in my Ministry Context?

Through God's grace and mercy, I understand who I am and know the God I serve. I realize that I am called to be on the frontline and to be used as a tool for God. Currently, I am exercising my philosophy in my ministry by serving as a Sunday School Superintendent. As such, I have a weekly opportunity to plan and teach a biblical lesson to the children. I believe that God has placed me where I need to be. Sometimes, I feel like I am not living up to my true potential, but then I realize that God is in control. Anxiety and fear are two powerful weapons that the enemy uses to deter us from our calling. Through the power of Scripture, I am able to combat weapons formed against me. I encourage all to read God's words:

> *Do not worry about your life, what you will eat, or about your body, what you will wear. Life is more than food, and the body more than clothes. Consider the ravens: They do not sow or reap, they have no storeroom or barn; yet God feeds them. And how much more valuable you are than birds! Who of you by worrying can add a single hour to his life? Since you cannot do this very little thing, why do you worry about the rest?* Luke 12:22-26

What I do well and not so well; my strengths and weaknesses

When I was younger, my relatives and friends always sought my advice during difficult times or traumatic situations. I believe that through life's experiences, humans develop a God-given ability to counsel and support one another during difficult times. I always pray that God uses me to comfort His people during challenging times. When I lost my wife, I realized that God was with me every step of the way; even when I could not see or feel His presence, He was guiding and carrying me in the right direction. This journey has helped me acquire the skills to minister to others. These are times that I can use to teach the Gospel and help others learn more about the good news of our Lord and Savior, Jesus

Christ. I think my weakness is not having patience with people who are not willing to listen and try God. However, during these times of weaknesses, I am reminded through Scripture that His *"grace is sufficient for you, for my power is made perfect in weakness. Therefore I will boast all the more gladly of my weaknesses, so that the power of Christ may rest upon me"* (2 Corinthians 12:9). I also assure others that a weakness is not a detriment and that through Christ, it is really a benefit.

What I would like to change? What needs to be Studied & Improved?

In the Episcopal Church, many of the traditional ways and customs are passed between generations. I believe that these traditional ways may have worked in the past, but if the church is going to move forward, we need to keep up with modern-day technology, such as having a web page for the church. When people are looking to relocate to an area and want to find a place of worship, their first resource is often the Internet. A web page will also help neighbors, friends, or anyone who is interested to learn about the various ministry groups in the church.

I would also like to see the Sunday school attendance improve. The Episcopal Church service normally lasts from 1 hour to 1.5 hours. This is not enough time to teach the congregation about God and his love for all of us. Sunday school and bible study are the best tools that a priest or pastor can use to build a biblically-based church. I believe that by studying an extra hour and sharing the Gospel about God's love, grace, and mercy, it will give members a chance to ask questions, share valuable information with others, and thus, will help the church family grow spiritually and physically. The good news is that the church, with good faith and consistency, can accomplish these goals. If we continue to have faith as small as a mustard seed, all things are possible, especially with God's help. This will lead to a prosperous and faithful church.

Chapter Four

The Inevitability of Grieving

For many, if not all humanity, grieving is an inevitable part of life. However, Christians are equipped with a belief system that supports the grieving process both in the moment of pain and in the envisioned future, where pain may no longer exist (Currier, Mallot, et al., 2013; Bray, 2013). The truths of the bible empower Christians to see their grief in healing light, bringing renewed meaning and purpose to both their suffering and their lives (Schultz, 2001).

According to McClatchey (2018), little is known about the experiences of widowed men and their children. Research about widowed men raising daughters was even more scarce. It is difficult for ministerial support staff and mental health professionals to assist this growing population with such limited knowledge.

During my wife's illness and after my loss, I looked to my personal relationship with God, the bible, prayer, my church, and my memories of her to help me cope with grief, as well as to raise my daughter. This literature review focuses on how an individual copes with the loss of a loved one through the support of scripture, the church, one's relationship with God, and creative methods for expressing and honoring one's grief.

Support of the Church

For those Christians who are experiencing the loss of a spouse or child, their church's support can offer a welcomed comfort. It is likely that many members of the community have suffered similar losses, and those who have shared grief are more equipped to help those who are suffering (Sittser, 1994). Sharing the lessons learned, or just providing company, is a helpful aid for those who feel overwhelmed by grief. A pitfall of despair is that it may turn into systemic depression, which can corrupt the rest of the individual's life. This is an example of grief that kills the spirit, and at the worst, can cause a total loss of faith or even suicide (MacArthur, 1998).

During this vulnerable time, the Body of Christ and the members of the church may offer their support through kind words, hugs, material assistance, or a simple prayer. Those who do not allow grief to corrupt them have reported that grief softened their hearts and helped them grow more compassionate towards the suffering of others. Pastors who specialize in grief counseling emphasize, "If we approach grieving Christians holistically, we will not wish to ignore mourners' physical needs any more than we would ignore their spiritual needs" (Culbertson, 1996, p. 229). This process entails the community of God to provide for the needs of their community. If a grieving member cannot find the will to shop for food or feed him or herself, the community will step in to help. As Christ said, *"For I was hungry, and you fed me. I was thirsty, and you gave me a drink. I was a stranger, and you invited me into your home"* (Matthew 24:35). If a church community displays this type of kindness and compassion towards a grieving member, these actions directly exemplify how the church regards Christ.

One of the church's main strengths is its ability to provide support to like-minded people. However, in this community, it is important to remember to honor the individual. For, "Each person's experience is his or her own, even if, on the face of it, the experience appears similar . . . Though suffering itself is universal, each experience of suffering is unique because each person who goes through it is unique" (Sittser, 1994). Because it is a fast-paced world, even those who have gone through similar suffering may be so far removed from it that they are callous towards the individual they are soothing. This emotion may come across as if the griever is being encouraged to speed up his or her process or see things from a different perspective. In his or her own time, the griever will come to a peaceful acceptance of the loss. Those in the church who are attempting to aid must be patient and gentle during this process (Lewis, 1961; Sittser, 1994; Culberton, 1996).

Taking Refuge in the Scriptures

Losing a spouse, child, or friend is difficult under any context, but for a Christian, many practical and philosophical tools are available for easing the effects of grief. There were many times during the loss of my wife that I was told to read the bible and pray, and everything would be fine. Honestly, like many Christians, I have always credited the bible as the voice and presence of God. According to evangelicals, Christians unanimously believe that the bible is how God communicates with us. According to Smith and Counsell (1991): "With the rise of Christian populations and the popularity of fundamental religious movements and

Scriptural study, therapists will probably be seeing more clients with whom the use of the bible can be a meaningful part of the therapy process" (p. 151).Lovinger (1996) makes a similar observation:

> *[T]he bible, which is often seen as a monolithic, impenetrable structure, is considered as much more flexible in meaning, and having qualities of humor, depth, and awareness of the human condition than many individuals are ordinarily aware of. If used properly; it can aid the therapeutic enterprise (p. 360).*

As Christians, we render ourselves to the Word of God, and each of us has to acknowledge that it is through the bible where you:

> *Must continue in the things which you have learned and been assured of, knowing from whom you have learned them, and that from childhood you have known the Holy Scriptures, which are able to make you wise for salvation through faith which is in Christ Jesus. All Scripture is given by inspiration of God, and is profitable for doctrine, for reproof, for correction, for instruction in righteousness, that the man of God may be complete, thoroughly equipped for every good work.* 2 Timothy 3:14-16.

Thus, we take refuge in the scripture, which further accelerates our drive to uplift His name and remind others to seek His word during times of grief and strife. As we know that we may not gather all as there may be that *"some boast*

in chariots and some in horses, but we will boast in the name of the LORD, our

God. They have bowed down and fallen, But we have risen and stood upright"

(Psalm 20:7-8).

According to Schultz (2001), the bible offers other benefits to support the

emotional burden of those who are experiencing an array of trials and tribulations:

> ***Teaching and training:*** 2 Timothy 3:16 tells us that God's Word is useful in teaching, training, and correcting us so that we will be able servants of God.
>
> ***Discernment and understanding****: When we study the bible and eat of its message, we gain an understanding and discernment about the world we live in (e.g., Psalm 111:10). The bible is not like a novel that we read once and talk it over with our friends. Rather, we continuously meditate on it so that we are able to recognize good from evil* (Hebrews 5:13).
>
> ***Comfort****:* The Psalmist tells us that God's Law is a source of comfort (119:52). Paul tells the Corinthians that prophecy (The Word of the Lord) *has a purpose: to comfort, strengthen and encourage believers* (1 Cor. 14:3).
>
> ***Hope:*** The bible is to be a comfort, but it is also builds hope— hope that God will deliver and keep his promises. Paul in

Romans 15 tells the reader that, *"For everything that was written in the past was written to teach us, so that through endurance and the encouragement of the Scriptures, we might have hope."* Psalm 119 expresses how the Psalmist finds hope in God's Word, and Isaiah suggests that *even the islands find hope in God's Law* (42:4).

The bible can cultivate hope and help ease the pangs of grief and despair when we evoke the memory of God's past assistance and when we "employ imagery to express the possibilities of new existence" (Guyette, 2003, p. 20): "In you our fathers put their trust; they trusted, and you delivered them. They cried to you and were saved; in you, they trusted and were not disappointed" (Ps. 22:4-5); "I remember the days of long ago; I meditate on all your works and consider what your hands have done" (Ps. 143:5). Sharing stories from the bible about God's involvement in the lives of his people can bring hope and expectation.

Acknowledging Eternity

Through the support of scripture, those who are grieving the loss of a loved one can hold the knowledge in their heart that their separation will be merely momentary in the scope of eternity. Barker (1973), editor of the NIV *Study Bible,* noted the following words in Paul's letter to the Thessalonians 4:13-18:

But we do not want you to be uninformed, brothers, about those who are asleep, that you may not grieve as others do who have no hope. For since we believe that Jesus died and rose again, even so, through Jesus, God will bring with him those who have fallen asleep. For this we declare to you by a word from the Lord, that we who are alive, who are left until the coming of the Lord, will not precede those who have fallen asleep. For the Lord himself will descend from heaven with a cry of command, with the voice of an archangel, and with the sound of the trumpet of God. And the dead in Christ will rise first. Then we who are alive, who are left, will be caught up together with them in the clouds to meet the Lord in the air, and so we will always be with the Lord (Barker, 1973).

I am a believer that this definitive passage of the bible outlines the Christian belief that all the faithful will live eternally in heaven, in celebration of the love that brought them into existence in the first place (Christmas, 2003).

The comfort that the belief in heaven supplies will not immediately cause the suffering of grief to dissipate, but over time, this belief has the potential to soothe the weary soul as a person patiently awaits reunion with loved ones. Christ made this promise, and he affirmed, *"Let not your hearts be troubled. Believe in God; believe also in me. In my Father's house are many rooms. If it were not so, would I have told you that I go to prepare a place for you?"*(John 14:1-30). Christ's sacrifice provided the bridge to eternity for the believers, and his descent into the underworld just prior to his resurrection is the bridge of light that the "sleeping ones" will walk on into paradise (Zonnebelt-Smeenge& De Vries, 1998).

For those who are grieving the loss of a spouse or child, this promise of eternity may seem to be not taken seriously. This response is partly because, being stuck in the realm of materiality, the concept of eternity has little meaning. Eternity is a concept of such significance that it simply dwarfs human understanding, which is hampered by the ever-present limitations of time, decay, and struggle. Imagining an eternity of peaceful union with the community of the beloved is difficult under the best of circumstances, but under the veil of grieving, this can seem insurmountable. In Deuteronomy 33:27, it is written, *"The eternal God is a dwelling place, and underneath are the everlasting arms."* God's eternal being is the construct in which all believers will live forever (Ziglar, 2004).

Eternity does not exist in the material realm without the loss of material flesh; the material and the spiritual realms are incompatible because of sin. The way through this paradox is faith in Christ, for if *"you confess with your mouth that Jesus is Lord and believe in your heart that God raised him from the dead, you will be saved . . .* For the Scripture says, *'Everyone who believes in him will not be put to shame'* (Romans 10:9-13). Shame is an eternity outside of the relationship of love, in which Christians question belief in Christ. Therefore, those who are grieving can remember that although they suffer for the moment, the expanse of eternity will be an everlasting experience of love with those they have lost (Dunn & Leonard).

This moment of everlasting eternity is expressed poignantly in Revelations. The prophet records the vision he was shown by Christ as,

> *Then I saw a new heaven and a new earth, for the first heaven and the first earth had passed away, and the sea was no more. And I saw the holy city, New Jerusalem, coming down out of heaven from God, prepared as a bride adorned for her husband. And I heard a loud voice from the throne saying, "Behold, the dwelling place of God is with man. He will dwell with them, and they will be his people, and God himself will be with them as their God. He will wipe away every tear from their eyes, and death shall be no more, neither shall there be mourning, nor crying, nor pain anymore, for the former things have passed away." And he who was seated on the throne said, "Behold, I am making all things new." (Revelation 21:1-27).*

In the final aspect of this vision, God makes all things new, and this is the promise that those who suffer the loss of their loved ones will embrace them anew in heaven. This embrace will last into eternity to which the current suffering will not even remain as memory and will be so far removed from the reality of heaven (Holmes, 1997).

However, it is important for Christians to seek to understand that the bible speaks of this realm of heaven united in a future tense, occurring only after the end of the material life. Although popular Christian belief is that their lost loved ones live now in heaven, Christian scholars remind the flock that the time is not yet. Van Biema (1998) quoted Bishop Wright:

> "In the bible, we are told that you die and enter an intermediate state. St. Paul is very clear that Jesus Christ has been raised from the dead already, but that nobody else has yet. Secondly, our physical state. The New Testament says that when Christ does return, the dead will experience a whole new life: not just our soul, but our bodies. And finally, the location. At no point do the resurrection narratives in the four Gospels say, "Jesus has been raised. Therefore we are all going to heaven." It says

that Christ is coming here to join together the heavens and the
earth in the act of new creation. (p. 1)".

Although a decrease in strictly bible-based teachings and awareness has occurred in recent years, giving way to popular belief and tradition, Christian leadership still emphasizes that God does exist.

> *The greatest example drawn from Jesus and promised to those who put their trust in him is resurrection from death. Believers have hope in their resurrection to life with him. Hinged on his resurrection from the dead, those who have put their trust in him can be confident of their own resurrection. The believers also have confidence that those who have died in him are equal heirs of the Kingdom of God (Benjamin, Vhumani, & Rantoa, 2013).*

Remembrance

A vitally important aspect of Christian grieving is remembrance. A sufficient understanding of life after the loss is required to honor remembrance without becoming frozen or obsessed by it. Remembrance entails choosing to hold on to the good memories of those who have been lost, such as a spouse (Oyebode& Owens, 2013; Hunter, 2007). Those who do not honor this process may attempt to forget all about the beloved to mitigate pain, but this lack causes more harm than good. A healthy sense of remembrance is ultimately valuing the time had with the loved one and keeping that love alive through memories. An unhealthy indulgence in this is enshrining loved ones through keeping their possessions frozen as if they were still alive (Christmas, 1993). Further, keeping the loved one alive to the degree that no other love can grow presents an imbalance that does not honor the loved one.

After a healthy period of grieving, it is natural to engage with new people and partake in new activities that will create new opportunities for love. If the grieving person holds on too long, he or she will miss out on their own life, and any learning and growing that may come from a loss will not occur or will not be shared with the community of believers surrounding them. This is a delicate balance that can only be achieved by the individual who pays close attention to her or his emotions (Marrocco, 1997). Riegel (2003) cited Jacques Derrida, who expressed this balance in *The Work of Mourning* as the following:

> *One should not develop a taste for mourning, and yet mourn, we must. We must, but we must not like it, that is, mourning itself, if such a thing exists: no to like or love through one's own tear but only through the other, and every tear is from*

the other, the friend, the living, as long as we ourselves are
living, reminding us, in holding like, to hold on to it. (p. 3)

A guide for balancing grieving and remembrance is a strong love of life, which may be difficult to cultivate during the period of loss (Wright, 2004). However, suppose the individual did cultivate a love of life prior to the loss. In that case, it will significantly help that person deal with the many conflicting and intense emotions associated with loss (Wiersbe, 1992).

Empowering Grief to Strengthen Relationship with God

Many books exist on the subject of Christian grieving, and these authors offer helpful insight into the process. Although the process of grieving is unique for each person, there are lessons to be gleaned from what grief has taught other believers. In the book *Good Grief,* Granger E. Westberg (1998) investigated the manner of emotions that complicate the Christian grieving process. Going through the normal stages of loss, Westberg emphasized that feelings of guilt may be involved in the grieving process.

At the very outset, we should make the distinction between "normal" guilt and neurotic guilt. Generally speaking, normal guilt is the guilt we feel when we have done something or neglected to do something...Neurotic guilt is feeling guilty all out of proportion to our own real involvement in a particular problem. (p. 43)

In the Christian grieving context, many Christians have harbored guilt for simply feeling sad, distressed, or angry because of their loss. Although Christians do believe in an eternity of life with their beloved Christ, this does not soothe the tumultuous emotions being born in physicality at the time of the loss. Thus, it is awful to feel guilty for going through normal emotions of loss, for all humanity is subject to the same psychological, and biological processes regardless of belief. Faith offers a support system for loss, but the loss is only experienced in the material realm (Hoos, 1998; Goldman, 2014).

A part of the normal process of grieving is denial, or the refusal to accept what has occurred. Christian counselors emphasize, "It may take you many months of working through your grief before you can finally accept death as a natural part of being human" (Shaw, 2002). It is helpful to remember and to accept this difficult truth is the passion of Christ. Christ's suffering was born from love, and God sent his Son so that Christians would know that their creator truly understands their sufferings. Christ did not avoid any of the difficult aspects of being human, and through his compassionate sacrifice, it is easier for humans to grieve (Wright, 2009).

For many Christians, losing a spouse or child causes an identity crisis. The beliefs and worldview that were once empowering now crumble under the weight of loss. Although this is a natural occurrence, the Christian faith is equipped to soothe those transitions. During the process of grieving, it is helpful for people to take some time away from normal responsibilities in order to rest and reset the foundations of their crumbled worldview. As Kim Thomas (2004) writes in *Finding Your Way Through Grief,*

> *It's okay to not do everything, and it's even okay to not do everything well. I may have to choose some things over others, letting go of some of the things I used to be able to handle... Her death has redefined my identity, and it will take time to become comfortable and confident in that... Right now there is a part of me that is unavailable for doing anything other than mourning and comforting myself.*

Thus, part of the grieving process is to be patient and compassionate with oneself. This entails knowing one's new limits, giving oneself the space to grieve, and not attempting to force situations and emotions that are harmful. In this context, fake joy is harmful, and others who attempt to force it onto a grieving person should be avoided as the process of grieving is naturally experienced (Neufeld).

Although suffering can be confusing, in the context of this earthly life as a training ground for eternity, suffering is merely a challenge that can draw one into a deeper relationship with the creator. Ecclesiastes 3: 1-2 affirms,

> *For everything there is a season, and a time for every matter under heaven: a time to be born, and a time to die; a time to plant, and a time to pluck up what is planted; a time to kill, and a time to heal; a time to break down, and a time to build up; a time to weep, and a time to laugh; a time to mourn, and a time to dance; a time to cast away stones, and a time to gather stones together; a time to embrace, and a time to refrain from embracing.*

This passage illustrates that there is a time for everything for those who are temporarily suffering from the loss of a loved one. Although God is outside of time,

His creation is not. What appears clear and right from God's perspective in eternity can appear wrong and meaningless from those mired in the web of time.

However, *"For now we see through a glass, darkly; but then face to face: now I know in part; but then shall I know even as also I am known"* (1 Corinthians 13:12). This passage from Corinthians relates that humanity does not and cannot see clearly while mired in the material realm. Although the material aspect of each person is limited and will decay, the spirit of the believer is eternal. For now, on the material plane, life appears chaotic and brutal, but from the perspective of heaven, suffering is the means by which the "wheat is separated from the chaff" (Zonnebelt-Smeenge& De Vries, 1997). Accepting the mystery of eternal life is essential for the Christian faith (White, 1997).

God has many mysterious attributes, but humans can use any experience in life to draw closer to that mystery, both in faith and trust (Culbertson, 1995). Many older people can look back on their lives and accept that the most difficult experiences they went through were some of the most transformative and strengthening phases of their life. In hindsight, these challenges may be appreciated, but the ends may not seem to justify the means in the moment of suffering. One Christian suffering a loss remarked, "As a nurse and a mother, I found that the hours between 1 a.m. and 6 a.m. can be very dark and frightening" (Neufeld, 2007). She turned to Psalm 30:5 to ease her dark night of the soul, which reads, *"weeping may stay during the darkness of night, but joy comes with the light of dawn"* (p. v). In this context, the bible verse encourages that the light will always come back, and the Psalms can offer comfort for those who are grieving (Lockwood, 2007).

The Power of Prayer

Those suffering the loss of loved ones may turn to God with everything in their hearts and minds, knowing they will not be rejected. During this time of grieving, the most powerful vehicle for strengthening one's relationship with God is prayer. Romans 8:26 guides the believer, "Likewise the Spirit helps us in our weakness. For we do not know what to pray for as we ought, but the Spirit himself intercedes for us with groanings too deep for words" (Barker, 1973). The groanings beyond words are the spirit expressing what it cannot understand, and this natural process of emotional release is healthy during times of grief. Prayer is a mystical conversation between Creator and created and cannot be explained in totality, which is where faith comes in (Lockwood, 2007). Even *"Jesus Himself would often slip away to the wilderness and pray"* (Luke 5:16). The Holy Scripture is our greatest source to utilize when defending how vitally important prayer is in our lives, especially during times of grief. Balarie (2015) provided the Scripture of Jesus praying and how we can apply it to our prayers:

1. *But Jesus often withdrew to lonely places and prayed. Lu. 5:16*

Getting alone gives our mind the white space it needs to conceptualize life-transforming spiritual needs.

2. *And going a little farther, he fell on his face and prayed, saying, My Father, if it be possible, let this cup pass from me; nevertheless, not as I will, but as you will.* Mt 26:39

Jesus was not afraid to ask for big deliverance. Our big God can handle big prayers. In fact, he loves a heart that believes by faith; he can do all things. Just ask it!

3. *My Father, if this cannot pass unless I drink it, your will be done.* Mt 26:42

Jesus knew God's will takes precedence over earthly will. When we pray, we should let our hearts convey needs, yet trust that God ultimately knows what we best need.

4. *And rising very early in the morning, while it was still dark.* Mk. 1:35

Jesus knew that seeing God first in his day sets the foundation of a day - in God. When we place our morning eyes on God, he gives our eyes sight on great strength in our day.

5. *Our Father in <u>heaven</u>, hallowed be your name.* Mt. 6:9

Jesus knew who he was talking to, do we? God tells us that the name of the Lord is a strong tower; the righteous can run into it and are safe (Prov 18:10). Do we believe this?

6. *And lead us not into temptation but deliver us from the evil one.* Mt. 6:13

Praying to be delivered from what has not already hit prevents your feet from getting swept out from under. Jesus teaches us to pray preemptively and for good reasons.

7. I praise you, Father, Lord of heaven and earth because you have hidden these things from the wise and learned and revealed them to little children. Yes, Father,
    for this was your good pleasure. Mt. 11:25-26

Jesus praised God for what man could easily find fault with. Praise God for the things you can't understand. When we know that a good God is over our bad problems, we find calm waters.

8. But I have prayed for you, Simon, that your faith may not fail. And when you have turned back, strengthen your brothers. Lu. 22:32
    Jesus knew the value of praying on behalf of faith. May we ask for more faith, so we can walk into the unseen with power, authority, and courage, just like Jesus.

9. I am praying for them. I am not praying for the world but for those whom you have given me, for they are yours. Holy Father, keep them in your name,
    which you have given me, that they may be one, even as we are one. Jo. 17:9

Jesus prayed for his beloved children. Let's pray that our heart, and the heart of all God's children, will endure, stay pure, and persevere together until the end, for this is God's will for us.

10. Jesus said, "Father, forgive them, for they do not know what they are doing." And they divided up his clothes by casting lots. Lu. 23:34

Jesus forgave when he could have cursed the world for his breath, labored pain, and agony. He didn't. Let's forgive those who cause us pain and agony, for what we will find is that forgiveness is what ends up causing us far less pain in the long run.

Prayer

It is our power.

It is our strength.

It is our direct connection to the greatest ruler of this earth.

It is our cosmic shift from selfish plans to God's plans.

It is our ability to be an influencer, a leader, and a worker in a kingdom that counts.

It is our ticket to our greatest needs being met in awe-inspiring ways.

It is our hope that confirms to our heart we have hope.

It is our peace that the creator is still creating.

It is our power found in uplifted hands and in the quietness of a solitary room.

It is our ability to call the Great Physician to a family member in need.

It is our emergency exit door for what the devil has already cooked up to destroy us.

It is our greatest weapon in a world that is building bigger and bigger weapons.

It is our lifeline when we feel we have lost all life.

It was one of Jesus' greatest tools,

shouldn't it be ours too? (n. p.)

Chapter Five

Methods

Christians turn to the church for their spiritual needs and comfort from grief. Blessed be the God and Father of our Lord Jesus Christ, the Father of mercies and God of all comfort, who comforts us in all afflictions so that we will be able to comfort those who are in any affliction with the comfort with which we ourselves are comforted by God. For just as the sufferings of Christ are ours in abundance, so also our comfort is abundant through Christ. 2 Corinthians 1:3-5.

This project is important to me because, when my wife died eight years ago from lung cancer, my daughter and I found nothing to help us as we experienced the grieving process. I would like to have information available when others find themselves in this situation. I feel this will be good for church members, as well as the community, to have a place of refuge and support.

Considering the support of the church in times of grief, with a specific interest in the needs of single fathers, the goal of this study was to explore and more fully understand the lived experience and perceptions of the support provided by the church for fathers raising daughters after the death of a spouse in the Protestant Episcopal Church in the Diocese of South Carolina. Ultimately, such a goal would lead the church to develop and implement grief ministry support systems within the Protestant Episcopal Diocese of South Carolina for single male parents raising daughters after the death of a spouse.

Research Design

A qualitative approach was chosen to identify and analyze the current perceptions of fathers raising daughters after the loss of a spouse. A qualitative approach is appropriate when the aim of the research is to obtain in-depth information about individuals' experiences and perceptions regarding a topic or phenomenon (Creswell, 2014). Because the research does not involve objectively and numerically measurable variables, a quantitative approach was considered but not selected for this study.

Reasons Why other Methods Might not be Appropriate

Creswell (2014) discussed phenomenological research as a design with roots in philosophy and psychology that explores the lived experiences of individuals who have shared a phenomenon. Interviews culminating in a case study were methods employed to gather data for this study. (Morse and McEvoy, 2014) concurred that a case study is appropriate when the aim of the research is to investigate or evaluate experiences, a setting, or a phenomenon shared by one or more individuals (Stake, 1995) discussed the case study as an appropriate design to use when studying a bounded phenomenon, one that is defined by activities within a specific time. In this study, the bounded phenomenon under investigation is support systems in the Protestant Episcopal Church in the Diocese of South Carolina for fathers raising daughters after losing a spouse.

Participant Selection, Context and Demographics

Participants: After all necessary approvals were obtained from the faculty of Ecumenical Theological Seminary and the Bishop of South Carolina, single male parents who were raising their daughters and were members of churches in theProtestant Episcopal Diocese of South Carolina and the Charleston County community were recruited to participate in semi-structured interviews. Recruiting efforts included information for newsletters in churches in the diocese and a special call to fathers sent to the alumni association of Voorhees College, which is affiliated with the Episcopal Church (See Appendix B).

Six widowers raising daughters contacted the researcher directly by phone or e-mail. The widowers between the ages of 35 and 57 whose wives had been deceased between one and five years. All were rearing adolescent girls, ages 12 to 17. During this initial contact, potential participants received information about the purpose of the study, what they would be asked to do, and a scheduled date and location for their interview. Each event was held on a Saturday at my church. The Bishop of the Diocese of South Carolina and my priest gave permission for the events to take place in the Parish Hall of the church that I attend.

Implementation of the Grief Ministry Event

One of the goals of this grief ministry project was to improve the way men communicate their feelings after losing a loved one. Staudacher (1991) offered that the low response of male participants to this grief ministry project could be because men have alternative ways to cope with grief, such as the following:

1. **Remaining silent:** keeping the pain private helps to protect against vulnerability in the form of tears, strong feelings, and sharing emotions.

2. **Grieving secretly:** grieving when no one can see to spare others from seeing, feeling, or experiencing that grief.

It is important to have the grief ministry event because there were few or no grief ministry support systems in churches. McClatchey (2018) emphasized that little is known about the experiences of widowed men and their children, and research about them is even more scarce.

The grief ministry event was conducted on Saturday, February 17, 2018, and Saturday, February 24, 2018. Three men were scheduled for each event. The interviews were individually scheduled between 9:00 a.m. and 12:00 p.m. in my church's Parish Hall. Each participant signed informed consent forms before the interview. Each interview lasted from 45 to 60 minutes. The interviews began with a prayer and followed the interview format as seen in Appendix C. After the completion of the interview, a closing prayer took place, and participants were thanked for their contributions to this grief ministry project.

Data Collection

Case studies use multiple sources of data or methods of data collection to investigate a specific case (Yin). The primary source of data for this study was semi-structured interviews with six single male parents from the Protestant Episcopal Diocese of South Carolina and the Charleston County community. A questionnaire, developed with the permission of the Bishop of the Diocese of Charleston, South Carolina, was the instrument used as the foundation for the semi-structured interviews of the focus group of the study participants at the church (See Appendix C).

The interviews were conducted in the Parish Hall, where participants felt comfortable and privacy was ensured. When participants arrived for the interview, they were asked to sign an informed consent form to confirm their willingness to participate in the study (See Appendix D). The informed consent form contained details about the study and information that they had the right to withdraw from the study at any time without consequences. Participants were informed that their data would be kept confidential and secure.

Each interview was semi-structured, meaning that the researcher followed a pre-constructed interview protocol and had the freedom and flexibility to probe for additional information and diverge from the protocol to discuss other relevant topics that emerged during the conversation (See Appendix E). Each interview of approximately one-hour was audio-recorded using a digital recording device. After the interview, the participants were thanked for their time and asked if they could be contacted later to answer potential follow-up questions or to verify their interview responses, a technique described by Creswell (2014) as member checking.

After data collection was complete, the audio-recorded interviews were transcribed into electronic text files. The audio recordings and text files were stored on a password-protected personal computer kept in a locked room to ensure data confidentiality.

Data Analysis Methods

Transcribed interviews and study documents were downloaded into NVivo, software designed to facilitate the organization and analysis of qualitative data. Data analysis involved following the thematic analysis procedures outlined by Braun and Clarke (2006). The robust qualitative data analysis technique is applicable to a variety of research designs, including case studies.

Braun and Clarke's (2006) thematic analysis technique involves six steps. In the first step, the researcher read and reread the interviews to gain an overall understanding of the data. The second step involved coding the interviews into basic units of meaning. Codes are labels assigned to sentences or words in the interview transcripts based on their meaning. In the third step, the codes created in Step 2 were grouped into an initial set of themes that explained the data in relation to the research question. Step four involved evaluating these initial themes to determine if any should be removed or further refined. In step 5, after the themes were adequately refined so that each theme was distinct and had sufficient supporting evidence, the themes were then defined and named. This step involved identifying the essence of each theme by reviewing the associated codes and assigning a name to each theme. The sixth and last step of the analysis involved writing the report of the themes.

The researcher described each theme in relation to the research question, and evidence from the interviews, such as quotations and excerpts, were presented in support of each theme. Additionally, the secondary data were triangulated with the interviews to corroborate the themes that emerged and to identify discrepancies between the data sources.

Chapter Six

Findings

The following research question guided this dissertation: What support systems are available in the Protestant Episcopal Church in the Diocese of South Carolina for fathers raising daughters after losing a spouse? Data were gathered in six semi-structured interviews conducted with men who were widowers raising daughters. Braun and Clarke's (2006) systematic data analysis method described in Chapter 5 was employed to generate the research findings that addressed the research question.

Data Analysis

The interview transcripts were read several times to ensure familiarity with the content (See Appendix E). Words or passages in each transcript that were relevant to the research question were assigned a code. Creswell discussed this process and suggested that codes may also be assigned to categorize the setting or characteristics of the participants, as well as the perceptions related to the phenomenon. Creswell noted that recording this type of detail, in particular, adds depth to the case study. Compiled, the coded text was categorized and labeled as themes with a short, descriptive name that reflected the content contained within. The researcher's interpretation of the themes became the foundation of the major findings, and interconnected themes are used by qualitative researchers to develop the narrative of the case study.

Results

The data analysis yielded four themes: a) the church did not provide official support programs, b) more church support desired, c) greater spiritual connection with God sought, and d) received support from women in their lives. The first theme directly addressed the research question. The final three themes were the result of further analysis of the data and highlighted the ways in which widowed men raising daughters sought help and support following the death of a spouse. Further analyses revealed that widowers raising daughters desired more support from their church, strengthened their spiritual connections with God, and turned to the women in their lives for help raising their daughters. Table 1 outlines the research question and related themes 2, 3, 4, with sub-themes.

Table 1 *Thematic Structure*

Research Question	Theme	Sub-Theme
What support systems are available in the Protestant Episcopal Church in the Diocese of South Carolina for fathers raising daughters after losing a spouse?	The church did not provide official support programs.	Did not know of any resources available
		No one offered or reached out with a support program.
How do widowers experience support following the death of a spouse?	More church support desired.	Faith-based counseling,
		guidance or support manual.
		More support for his children.
		More individual support and connections.
		More than individual support.
	Greater spiritual connection with God sought.	Faith
		Prayer
	Received support from	Female friends

women in their lives.	provided support for daughter.
	Significant other provided support for daughter(s).
	Sister(s) provided support for daughter(s).

Theme 1: The Church did not Provide Official Support Programs

In direct answer to the research question, the consensus of the participants was that the Protestant Episcopal Church in the Diocese of South Carolina did not officially provide support programs for fathers raising daughters after losing a spouse? Two identifiable sub-themes emerged in the data:

Participants did not know of any resources available. Four men of the six men interviewed stated that they did not know of any resources their church provided to help them or provide support after their wives died. Participant 2 said that there was no support, but "that's something that I wished that there was more of back then." This was echoed by Participant 5, who said, "No, the church that I'm currently serving does not offer any kind of support group. There's not any support

85

system available at the church." He elaborated, "Currently, there are no resources provided at the church for widowers like myself who lost someone, a spouse. There are no resources."

No one offered or reached out with a support program. Four of the six participants also discussed how, in addition to no support programs in their church for widowers, no one reached out to them with a program. Participant 2 said, "There wasn't really anything set up or even really offered to me," and Participant 4 said, "I can tell you, I don't know of any, nor have learned of one through my denomination." Participant 3 added, "As far as any particular programs, I think if we had any in place, I believe that we'd be introduced to them," and "that didn't happen."

Theme 2: Desired More Church Support

Overall, the participants voiced their desire for more church support. Because they did not receive any official support from their churches, participants offered various ideas for the support that they would like to have seen or ways that their church could improve in the future. Five discernable sub-themes emerged that were related to theme 2:

Wanted faith-based counseling: Two participants. Participant 3 and Participant 6 wanted more counseling services from their church. Participant 3 said that "I believe more in grief counseling for me, and for my daughters to have that transition period. Going from all of a sudden, having a family to all of a sudden, no one is departed. I would love it if they had a program in place to bridge that gap that's gone. Yeah, I definitely would've (...) that would've been something that would've been in place, that would've been great".

Participant 6 said that he wanted "just general counseling. There are not a lot of places outside of structured counseling services where you can generally sit down and express how you feel without being judged that the infrastructure of a school will mandate reporters."

Wanted more individual support and connections: Participants 4 and 6 also wanted more support from other parishioners. They also expressed having more support in the way of individual person-to-person connection to support them after the death of their spouses. Participant 4 said, "I don't know if this is going to make sense. I think when we do church right, when we truly have a community within our churches, when we've built those relationships (…) I think back when I was a kid, my parents' friends were all from the church that we attended. When we did something as a family on a Saturday night, it was normally with one or two of those church people. I think it's about building community and relationship, and they already exist in the church".

Similar to the thoughts of Participant 4, Participant 6 stated, "Churches can be so powerful. But at the end of the day, just individuals that you have there that have a vested interest in cultivating the church."

Wanted more support for his children: Three participants desired more support from the church for their children after their mother died. Participant 1 said, "I grew up in a church where the catechism is very spot-on teaching (sic)" and wanted that for his children, but also wanted help in the way of childcare, too.

Anticipant 4 wanted support specifically for his daughter in whatever form that might take. He said,

> *"Somehow, I don't know if it's through (...) ladies' dinners, or ladies' fellowship day, or ladies' let's go shopping, I don't know what that would look like, but can build ... have those relationships where...you know the youth of the church are connecting at a different level than it just being oh, Ms. Jones on Sunday morning, Hi Ms. Jones, how are you? Whether they have some kind of...whether they go to an amusement park or they meet once a month for dinner at Red Robin, so there's a relationship there. If the relationship is there, then I think those young ladies would gravitate to those women with whom they probably already have a very good relationship".*

Participant 6 was more interested in some kind of peer counseling for his children. He stated:

"Peer counseling is something that I've actually talked to the church in regards because lots of times, kids want to talk to other kids about certain things. With that, you have adults that work in a church that kids see all the time that they become accustomed to, that they trust".

Wanted more than individual support: Half of the men felt that they received support from members in their church on an individual, personal level, but they desired more support in the way of formal groups or similar. Participant 2 said that there were groups at the church, but there were no support groups like what he would have wanted. He spoke about bible study groups and young adult groups that his church offered and nothing in the way of support groups for parishioners. Participant 3 felt supported by parishioners in his church when his wife first died, but that waned after a while. He said,

"I don't know of any support that they have in place. I know we have when everything first…When my wife had first passed away and everything, they were very helpful in different ministries in supporting and calling and, you know, just being a supporting cast".

Participant 4 also felt like the support that he was given was very helpful, but not quite as much as he wanted. He said, "it wasn't that they were not [there for me], just not enough." He felt that they were there for him, though he just wanted more from them during this difficult time in his life.

Theme 3: Sought Greater Spiritual Connection with God

All participants described how they leaned on and drew strength from their connection with God. Their relationship with God was as important for their healing as support from the church. Theme 3 contained two sub-themes:

Faith: Two men described the importance of faith in their lives, especially after the loss of their wives. Participant 2 said that he is "a firm believer that having faith, whether or not you go to church every Sunday, or have a large group of individuals that you meet on a Wednesday from church, or anything like that." For him, this faith could be expressed in different ways, and that no matter what, these expressions of faith were helpful. Participant 3 simply said, "If it wasn't for my faith, I tell you what, I don't know what we would've done."

Prayer: All six participants described how important prayer was when they lost their wives. They described the impact of their own prayers and the prayers that others had on their lives. Participant 1 described the women in his life as "prayer warriors" but said that he prays as well. He includes himself and his family and his own prayers but often prays for others outside of his family as well.

Participant 2 described how prayer had a calming effect. He stated, "It did really kind of help calm (…) me down. It was like me being able to kind of just release and get out everything that just stayed bottled up throughout the day." He elaborated that,

> *"I'm just the type of individual that prays. So, I don't know if I would say that there has been an effect on it, since I raised my daughter, except that, like I said, there were times for sure that it really helped me get things off my chest".*

He also enjoyed prayer with his daughter, stating that it was a way for them to maintain their bond. Participant 6 also enjoyed the time that he set aside with his children for prayer. He said:

> *"One of the things that I've done in my household is to make prayer primary. Church has always been a staple. Every Sunday, no matter what we did, we went to church to attend*

services. I am not as consistent going to church, but we're very consistent in prayer and the infrastructure of what church really is. One of the things that we do nightly and in the morning is to have prayer with my kids. I actually wanted my kids to understand why we pray. (...) me praying with my sons and daughter. What we do twice a week is we all sit down, and they all bring a bible verse. What they have to do with the bible verse is elaborate on it. What do they bring out of it? What can they implement in the day-to-day that they're doing, going to school, social media, different things that they're seeing and hearing? How is it affecting them? Initially, they met me with some resistance because they really didn't understand".

Participant four felt like the prayers of others were the most helpful and powerful for him. He said:

"I mean, my life, and my prayer life, has always been a part of who I am. I really feel the prayer from others got me through this stuff. I mean [I] can sit and pray all [I want], but having the family, my mom had already passed at this point, but my dad was alive and the prayer that he would send, my extended family, those surrogate mothers that are out there, and those older aunts and late aunts were out there. I mean, I could feel the support of my people praying to get me through this. I could absolutely feel it. (...) I pray for strength, guidance, and direction absolutely every day. I've never done this before. Never done this before, and being a single father, definitely never done that before, and as you know, there's not a lot of us out there".

He said that he prays for his daughter, that he's making the right decisions for her, and that God is with her throughout the day when he can't be with her himself.

Theme 4: Received Support from Women in their Lives

One way that four participants have found support following the death of their spouses is from their female friends and family. Men described the ways in which the women in their lives stepped in to help them with their daughters. This support came from the women in their lives, both family and friends, and also from their new significant others.

Female friends provided support for daughter(s). Participant 4 received help from his parents' friends. He has women in his life who have helped him, and one woman, in particular, has been very helpful with his daughter. His parent's best friend, who is like an aunt, helped his daughter with things like bra shopping when she became a teenager and the time came. He also relied on the other strong women in his daughter's life. He said,

"There are some things dads just don't know when it comes to little girls, and fortunately for [my daughter], she's a good student, she's athletic, so she's involved in a lot of things, and she had some pretty powerful women, strong women who looked after her and made sure those female worries and concerns were taken care of. One of her best friend's moms is the health teacher at the high school. So when it came for menstrual cycles and those stomach aches or those cramps would happen, and in the middle of third hour kind of thing [she] had a mother figure there that just loves [her] to no end, and she was there to take care of her".

Further, he explained, "I just had a lot of women that would come forward and help me out. But I truly, truly was blessed."

Participant 5 relied on women in his church for advice about raising daughters. He stated,

"The church has supported me by giving me some good advice about raising daughters. The church women have talked to my daughter about certain things, and if she needed any assistance, that he should call them. So the church was there to give me some positive feedback when they see that there was a question. So, the women in the church have really helped me as far as raising my daughter".

Significant other provided support for daughter(s). Participants 4 and 5 also relied on help from their current significant others. Participant 4 said,

"My significant other, who actually I've known for many years, was at one time [my daughter's] Girl Scout leader. They used to do a lot of activities. Well, they still do a lot of activities, but she was another person that [my daughter] would go to without hesitation. Both of these ladies, because I tell you, in some regards it really made [my daughter] a strong, independent young lady, because she's not afraid to go out and seek guidance from others.

This was the case for Participant 5 as well. He said, "Then my friend, my female friend who I've been dating, she's been helping me out just talking to her, and encouraging her to do well; Not only in her surroundings but to do well in school."

Sister(s) provided support for daughter(s). Other men described how the women in their family provided them with support. Participant 1 asks his mom and sisters for advice sometimes. His sister is frequently in the area for work, and "so once a month she comes down brings her son who's about four. Sometimes she brings my other sister." Participant 5 turned to his sister when his daughter became a teenager. He said,

"Well, my daughter recently just turned 13. So, she was at a stage now, where here...she was starting to develop as a woman. So at that stage of her life, I needed help with her...the change and when her cycle began. So I had to reach out to my sister, who also has a daughter, who is a year older than my daughter. My family member has really helped me out.

The relationship of themes, sub-themes, and relationship questions are

outlined in Figure 1

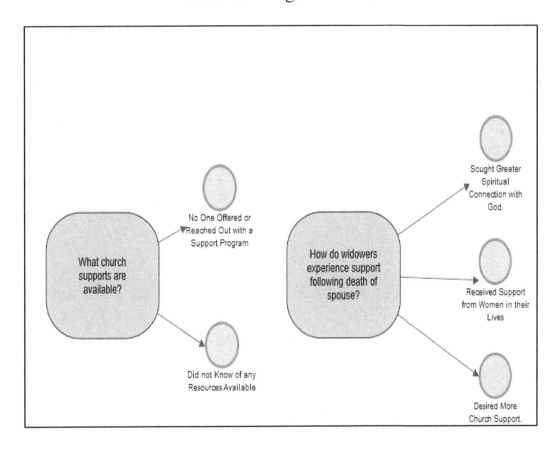

Figure1 Relationship between research question, themes, and subthemes

Limitations and Delimitations

In this study, I analyzed the support systems that are available in the Protestant Episcopal Church in the Diocese of South Carolina for fathers raising daughters after losing a spouse. However, as with all research studies, there are limitations and delimitations. A limitation is an "uncontrollable threat to internal validity" (Ellis & Levy, 2009). In other words, a limitation cannot be controlled by the researcher. Careful researchers must acknowledge the limitations of a study for their readers; however, although the researcher cannot control a study's limitations, they may be able to minimize such limitations. Recognizing limitations can alert future researchers who wish to replicate the study to understand constraints that may arise.

Limitations: The following characteristics describe the limitations of this study:

- Many factors may influence the responses of participants in relation to support of the church for fathers raising daughters following the death of a spouse, including internal and external factors, such as the role of church and/or diocesan leadership, the availability of counseling staff, the social structure or activity level of the church, and other parochial or community factors.

- All subjects in the study were volunteers. This meant that they could withdraw from the study at any time, thereby reducing the sample size.

- This study had a low response rate. A total of six men participated in this study. This may have been because there is a limited population of widowers raising a daughter(s).

- Other Protestant Dioceses of South Carolina may differ according to various economic, ethnic, racial, or social characteristics.

- The results of this research may not be generalized to other Protestant Episcopal Dioceses in other parts of the United States or to other local or regional religious organizations.

- The researcher's assumption was that all participants were truthful in their responses. Given the sensitive nature of the interview questions, participants may not have fully disclosed their experiences in the interview process.

Delimitations: A delimitation is "a systematic bias intentionally introduced into the study design or instrument by the researcher" (Price & Murnan, 2004). Delimitations can be controlled by the researcher and help to define its boundaries. In presenting the delimitations of a study, the researcher enhances the replicability of the study, as future researchers gain an understanding of the study's boundaries and may suggest ways that similar studies may be extended by varying choices of delimitations. The following characteristics describe the delimitations of this study:

- This study was conducted in only one Protestant Episcopal Diocese of South Carolina. Doing so automatically limited the sampling pool for this study and the number of potential participants.
- The focus of the initial questionnaire and interview was limited to experiences related to the support of the church in issues of fathers raising daughters following the death of a spouse.
- This research involved only widowers raising a daughter(s). The study did not include widows, nor widows or widowers raising

boys, nor parents of either gender who were single by reason other than the death of a spouse.

Summary

Results of this qualitative research study based on semi-structured interviews with six widowed men raising daughters were presented in this chapter. Overall, the results showed that their church provided no specific support systems for men in this unique circumstance. Participants indicated that they desired more support from their church, both in terms of individual connections with other parishioners and in terms of group support systems. They described the kinds of support systems that they would like to see in place for widowers and their children. As there was no formal support, participants described how they drew on their faith in God to find strength during this difficult time in their lives. They also leaned on the women in their lives, especially as their daughters came of age and needed female role models. The concluding chapter in this dissertation includes the implications of these findings, reflections, and recommendations for future studies.

Chapter Seven

Conclusions, Reflection, and Recommendations

In many cases, single parents lack the resources and social support system necessary for raising a child. Approximately 13.6 million single parents in the United States are raising more than 21 million children (KIDS COUNT Data Center, 2016). Although social systems have rapidly accepted single-parent, female-led families, single fathers remain a rare occurrence and therefore have more difficulties in accessing social support.

The Protestant Episcopal Church in the Diocese of South Carolina has about 22,000 baptized members spread across the east coast side of the state. The bishop of the diocese acknowledged that the church is an integral part of society and is advantageously positioned to solve the challenges of single parenting and grief management. Grief can affect the entirety of the Christian mission. When a person dies, the Christian belief is that the individual has transitioned into a better existence. However, the bereavement causes tremendous grief and sadness for the Christian family experiencing the loss of a loved one. The church's primary goal is to bring hope in such a period that may be accompanied by disillusionment and despair.

This case study explored the lived experience and perceptions of six single men regarding support systems available in the Protestant Episcopal Church in the Diocese of South Carolina for fathers raising daughters after losing a spouse. Findings pointed to a lack of formal, faith-based support programs. Data from this study indicated that participants desired more support from their church, both in terms of individual connections with other parishioners but also in terms of group support systems such as faith-based counseling and more support for individuals throughout the grief process, as well as more support for parenting after the loss of a spouse.

Semi-structured interviews revealed ways that the participants coped with the loss of a spouse and the role of a single parent. In search of comfort and support, the participants were able to rely on their faith and prayer to establish a greater spiritual connection to God. Further, participants described support provided by female family members and friends, especially the assistance as their daughters came of age and needed female role models.

This study further illustrated that for many, if not all, grieving is an inevitable part of life. However, Christians are equipped with a belief system that supports the grieving process both in the moment of pain and in the envisioned future, where pain may no longer exist. Losing a spouse, child, or friend is difficult under any context, but for a Christian, many practical and philosophical tools are available for easing the effects of grief. The participants in this study identified their tools as the bible, the church, one's relationship with God, and support from family and friends, especially the women in their lives. They expressed that having a grief ministry support system at their church would have been a welcomed comfort. If it is the role of a church community to display this type of kindness and compassion towards a grieving member, then these actions directly exemplify how the church regards Christ. One of the church's main strengths is its ability to provide support to like-minded people. Those in the church who are attempting to aid a grieving member must be patient and gentle during this process.

Unanticipated Discoveries

The men in this study asserted that during a time of grieving, the most powerful vehicle for strengthening one's relationship with God was prayer. They recommended to those suffering the loss of a loved one(s) to turn to God with everything in their hearts and minds, knowing they will not be rejected. One of the participants expressed the need for the church to provide guidance or a support manual. Others relayed that their daughters taught them more than anyone. Additionally, one individual enjoyed prayer with his daughter and highlighted it as being therapeutic for the both of them.

Reflections

The truths of the bible empower Christians to see their grief in a healing light, bringing renewed meaning and purpose to both their suffering and their lives.

Losing a spouse, child, or friend is difficult under any context, but for a Christian, many practical and philosophical tools are available for easing the effects of grief. Through the support of scripture, those who are grieving the loss of a loved one can hold the knowledge in their heart that their separation will be merely momentary in the scope of eternity. Loss and grieving is unavoidable in this life as a natural extension of the original sin. However, in its natural expression, grief has a healing power that can strengthen an individual's relationship with God and can allow a person to love life. This love will transcend death, especially as loved ones are reunited in the new Earth. Outside of time, God extends His embrace for all those who receive his love. In the context of the all-embracing love, God offers the losses suffered in this life that may be endured. Because of His love, we can move forward.

Recommendations for Future Studies

This study analyzed the support systems that are available in the Protestant Episcopal Church in the Diocese of South Carolina for fathers raising daughters after losing a spouse. The following recommendations are offered to extend this scope of research in future studies:

1. Demographically, this study was based on responses from widowers raising a daughter(s). Considering the fact that there are more single parents raising children of all genders, examining the perspective of both single mothers and fathers would provide more insight into how to best develop a grief support ministry for single parents experiencing loss.

2. This study was conducted to a limited population only in one Protestant Episcopal Diocese of South Carolina. Similar studies could be expanded to other Christian and non-Christian denominations and other geographic areas.

3. Future research could explore the grieving process and lived experience of the children being raised by a single parent after the death of a spouse. What sources of comfort and support are available at the church, family, friends, and community?

4. Data gathered by research that focuses on the insights of older children who were raised by a single parent might provide a foundation for the development of appropriate support systems in the church and community.

5. Finally, the church is urged to develop and implement faith-based programs for single parents and children in their care that includes guidance and comfort during periods of grief and assistance for meeting the needs of children at various stages of their physical, social, and spiritual growth.

References

Barker, K.L. (Ed.) (1973). *NIV Study Bible Zondervan*. Grand Rapids:Zondervan.

Being a single parent(2015). *Children's Trust of South Carolina. Scchildren.org.* Retrieved **5** October 2016, from https://scchildren.org/building_strong_families/understand_all_kinds_of_fa milies/single_parents.

Balarie, K. (2015). *Ten Bible verses that teach us how Jesus prayed*. Retrieved from https://www.crosswalk.com/blogs/kelly-balarie/10-bible-verses-how-jesus-prayed.html

Braun, V., & Clarke, V. (2006). Using thematic analysis in psychology. *Qualitative Research in Psychology, 3*(2), 77-101. DOI: 10.1191/1478088706qp063oa

Children living in single-parent families (Decennial Census Series) | KIDS COUNT Data Center. (2015). *Datacenter.kidscount.org.* (2015-2016), from http://www.datacenter.kidscount.org/data/tables/2897-children-living-in-single-parent-families-decennial-census-series#detailed/2/any/false/133,11,1,42/any/5998.

Christmas, A.E. (2003). *Who needs me? The Christian answer for grief.* Conshohocken, PA:: Infinity.

Creswell, J. W. (2014). *Research design: qualitative, quantitative, and mixed methods approach (4th ed.)*. Thousand Oaks, CA: Sage.

Culbertson, P. (2000). *Caring for God's people: Counseling and Christian wholeness.* Minneapolis: Augsburg Fortress.

Dunn, B. & Leonard, K. (2004). *Through a season of grief: Devotions for your journey from mourning to joy.* Nashville: Thomas Nelson.

Ellis, T. &Levy, Y. (2009). Towards a guide for novice researchers on research methodology: Review and proposed methods. *Issues in Informing Science and Information Technology* (5), 323-337.

Guest, G., Bunce, A., & Johnson, L. (2006). How many interviews are enough? An experiment with data saturation and variability. *Field Methods, 18*(1), 59-82. DOI: 10.1177/1525822X05279903

Homeless single dad devoted to daughter. (2015). *Charleston Gazette-Mail.* Retrieved 3 October 2015, from http://www.wvgazettemail.com/article/20140614/GZ05/140619705

Hoos, C. (2016). How can I have faith after losing my son? *Power to change.* Retrieved from: http://powertochange.com/discover/faith/havefaith/.

Holmes, B.M. (2014). *What are you crying about? Defeating grief for Christians (and other believers).* Holmes House Press.

Jackson, M. (2015). *It is well with my soul.* Recorded vocal retrieved from https://youtu.be/4FywLpFRcgk

Jonsson, P. (2000). Churches give single moms a warmer shoulder. *Christian Science Monitor, 92* (211), 1-3.

Johnson, E.L. (2007). *Foundations for soul care: A Christian psychology proposal.*Downers Grove, IL: IVP Academic.

KIDS COUNT Data Center(2016). *Annual report.* Baltimore, MD: Project of the
    Annie E. Casey Foundation.

Lawrence, M. (2009). Retrieved from https://www.dioceseofsc.org/about/.

Lewis, C.S. (1961). *A Grief observed.* New York: Faber and Faber.

Lockwood, D.R. (2007). Until we meet again. *Christianity Today,* 23 Oct. 2007.
    Retrieved from:
    http://www.christianitytoday.com/ct/2007/october/41.98.html

MacArthur, J. (1998). *The glory of heaven.* Wheaton, IL: Crossway Books.

McClatchey, I. S. (2018). Fathers raising motherless children: Widowed men
    give voice to their lived experiences. *Omega: Journal Of Death & Dying,*
    76(4), 307-327. doi:10.1177/0030222817693141

Marrocco, N.(1997). *Death, grief, and Christian hope.* Winona, MN: Saint Mary's
    Press.

McMinn &T.R. Phillips (Eds.), *Care for the soul: Exploring the intersection of*
    psychology and theology (pp. 254-275). Downers Grove, IL: InterVarsity
    Press.

Morse, A. L., & McEvoy, C. D. (2014). Qualitative research in sport
    management: Case study as a methodological approach. *The Qualitative*
    Report, 19, 1–13.

Neufeld, J. (2007). *Grief: Finding the candle of light.* Gonzalez, FL: Energion.

Powell, P. (2014). Against all odds: History of Saint Andrew's Parish Church,
    Charleston, 1706–2013. Bloomington, IN: Westbow Press.

Price, J. &Murnan, J. (2004) Research limitations and the necessity of reporting them, *American Journal of Health Education*, 35:2, 66-67, DOI: 10.1080/19325037.2004.10603611.

Rank, M. (1985). Free to Grieve: Healing and encouragement for those who have suffered. Bloomington, IN: Bethany Houses.

Riegel, C. (2003). Writing grief: Margaret Laurence and the work of mourning. Winnipeg: University of Manitoba Press.

Shaw, N. (2002). *The valley of tears (eBook): A journey through grief.* Vereeniging in Gauteng province, South Africa: Christian Art Publishers.

Sittser, J.L.(2004). *A grace disguised: How the soul grows through loss.* Grand Rapids, MI: Zondervan.

Schultz, R. (2001). Responsible hermeneutics for wisdom literature. In M.R.

SiSwati, B., Magezi, V. &Letšosa, R., 2013, 'Bereavement healing ministry amongst Abaluyia: Towards a "circle for pastoral concern" as a healing model,' *In die Skriflig/In Luce Verbi*47(1), Art. #663, 11 pages. http://dx.doi.org/10.4102/ids.v47i1.663

Smith, T. L. (2007). *Darkness is my closest friend: Using the psalms of lament to address grief issues.* Paper presented at the North American Association of Christians in Social Work, Dallas, TX.

Spafford, H. G. (1876). *It is well with my soul.* First published in Gospel Songs, Number 2, by Sankey and Bliss.

Stake, R. E. (1995). *The art of case study research*. Thousand Oaks, CA: Sage.

Thomas, K. (2004). *Finding your way through grief.* Eugene: Harvest House.

Van Biema, D. (2007). Christians wrong about heaven, says Bishop. *TIME,* 7 Feb. 2008. Retrieved from:
http://content.time.com/time/world/article/0,8599,1710844,00.html

Westberg, G.E. (2011). *Good grief.* Minneapolis: Fortress Press.

Wiersbe, D.W. (1992). *Gone but not lost: Grieving the death of a child.* Grand Rapids, MI: BakerBooks.

White, J.R. (1997). *Grieving: Our path back to peace.* Grand Rapids, MI: Baker Books.

Wright, H.N. (2004). *Experiencing grief.* Nashville: B & H Publishing Group.

Wright, H.N. (2009). Reflections of a Grieving Spouse: The Unexpected Journey from Loss to Renewed Hope. Eugene, OR: Harvest House.

Yin, Y. K. (2013). *Case study research: Design and methods* (5th ed.). Thousand Oaks, CA: Sage.

Ziglar, Z. (2004). *Confessions of a Grieving Christian.* Nashville: B & H Publishing Group.

Zonnebelt-Smeenge, S. J. R.N, & De Vries, R.C. (1998). *Getting to the other side of grief: Overcoming the loss of a spouse.* Grand Rapids, MI: Baker Books.

Zonnebelt-Smeenge, S. J. R.N, & De Vries, R.C.(2006). *Traveling through Grief: Learning to live again after the death of a loved one.* Grand Rapids, MI: Baker Books.

Appendix A: Family and Community Indicators

Children in single-parent families by state

Total number of children and percentage

United States	24,689,000	35	Missouri	457,000	35
Alabama	412,000	40	Montana	63,000	30
Alaska	54,000	31	Nebraska	132,000	29
Arizona	569,000	37	Nevada	248,000	39
Arkansas	259,000	39	New Hampshire	78,000	31
California	2,996,000	34	New Jersey	612,000	32
Colorado	367,000	31	New Mexico	193,000	41
Connecticut	252,000	34	New York	1,450,000	36
Delaware	80,000	42	North Carolina	811,000	37
District of Columbia	of57,000	53	North Dakota	47,000	29
Florida	1,547,000	40	Ohio	942,000	38
Georgia	930,000	39	Oklahoma	317,000	36
Hawaii	91,000	32	Oregon	269,000	33
Idaho	108,000	26	Pennsylvania	905,000	35
Illinois	965,000	34	Puerto Rico	440,000	59
Indiana	539,000	36	Rhode Island	80,000	39
Iowa	202,000	29	South Carolina	432,000	43
Kansas	212,000	31	South Dakota	60,000	30
Kentucky	328,000	35	Tennessee	523,000	37
Louisiana	488,000	47	Texas	2,416,000	36
Maine	86,000	35	Utah	168,000	19
Maryland	466,000	36	Vermont	41,000	35
Massachusetts	425,000	32	Virginia	552,000	31
Michigan	762,000	36	Washington	457,000	30
Minnesota	348,000	28	West Virginia	130,000	37
Mississippi	322,000	47	Wisconsin	408,000	33

Appendix B: Recruiting Participants

Special Call to Fathers who are or have raised daughters:

Voorhees Alumnus Seeks Research Input

As a father, raising a daughter(s) alone can oftentimes be a difficult yet joyful journey. Alumnus Bruce D. Johnson is looking for fathers who are raising or have

 raised a daughter(s) to participate in a research project by attending a grief ministry event to discuss how you have utilized Scripture and the church as a support system, as well as your thoughts and experiences as a father raising a daughter. If you are willing to participate, contact Johnson at either brucedj36@yahoo.com

Bruce Johnson was born and reared in Charleston, South Carolina, by his parents, Mr. and Mrs. Alfred and Bernice Johnson. He was the youngest son of five children, and he often spent his free time with his friends in the neighborhood. His Grandmother always ensured that he attended church every Sunday, where his love for God first began. When he was younger, he often received recognition for his time spent on the field, engaging in football, basketball or baseball. After high school, he worked for the United Parcel Service (UPS) for more than twenty-three years, where he was on of the first in his center to receive a baccalaureate degree while working for the company.

Bruce attended Voorhees College, a Historically Black College and University (HBCU) in Denmark, South Carolina. Soon after, he married his beloved late spouse, Dr. Maria L. Goodloe-Johnson. They later relocated to Seattle, Washington. During this time, he had a spiritual awakening that led him to enroll and attend Seattle U, a private Jesuit University in downtown Seattle, Washington. There he received his Master of Arts Degree in Pastor Studies. Soon after, he and his family relocated to Detroit, Michigan, where he earned his Doctor of Ministry Degree from Ecumenical Theological Seminary.

After Bruce's wife, the late Dr. Maria E. Goodloe-Johnson, went from labor to reward and received her heavenly wings, he relocated to South Carolina to rear his daughter with the help of his family and friends. Bruce and his daughter attended the church where his Father, Grandmother and Great Grandmother were members and worshipped. Even though he had lost the love of his life he, in turn, gained the help and support of so many others, for which he is eternally grateful.

Synopsis

Single fathers remain a rare occurrence and therefore have more difficulties in accessing social support. According to the U.S. Bureau of Statistics, about two million single fathers live in the United States. This accounts for about 17% of all the single parents in the United States. This study aimed to explore and more fully understand the lived experience and perceptions of the support provided by the church for fathers raising daughters after the death of a spouse in the Protestant Episcopal Church in the Diocese of South Carolina.

This study's population consisted of six single male parents who responded to an invitation to be interviewed about the support systems that are available in their church. The data analysis yielded four themes: a) the church did not provide official support programs, b) more church support was desired, c) greater spiritual connection with God was sought, and d) participants received support from women in their church, family, and community. Although the participants reported no official church-affiliated support programs, the widowed men raising daughters sought help and support following the death of a spouse in their faith, prayer, and assistance of women in the church, family, and community.

Recommendations for future study included an expanded study of church support for single parents of both genders in a broader denominational, social, economic, and geographic context. Further, a goal of extended research could be to develop and implement faith-based programs offering guidance and comfort to families during the period of grief and assistance to single parents for meeting the needs of their children.

Made in the USA
Monee, IL
10 July 2021

73310300R00072